Special Problems

TIME LIFE BOOKS ®

Life World Library
Life Nature Library
Time Reading Program
The Life History of the United States
Life Science Library
Great Ages of Man
Time-Life Library of Art
Time-Life Library of America
Foods of the World
This Fabulous Century
Life Library of Photography
The Time-Life Encyclopedia of Gardening
Family Library
 The Time-Life Book of Family Finance
 The Time-Life Family Legal Guide
The American Wilderness

LIFE LIBRARY OF PHOTOGRAPHY

Special Problems

BY THE EDITORS OF TIME-LIFE BOOKS

TIME-LIFE BOOKS, NEW YORK

ON THE COVER: The brutal heat of the desert and the bitter cold of a snowstorm are but two of the special problems photographers must face. Allen Dutton's picture of the desert near Yuma, Arizona, was taken in December. But he had to shoot it at dawn to avoid the fierce sun that bakes the land even in winter. The picture of snow on the door of a shed by Minor White was shot after a five-day blizzard in upper New York State. The 10° temperature made the metal of the camera so cold White had to shift it from hand to hand, even though he was wearing gloves.

Contents

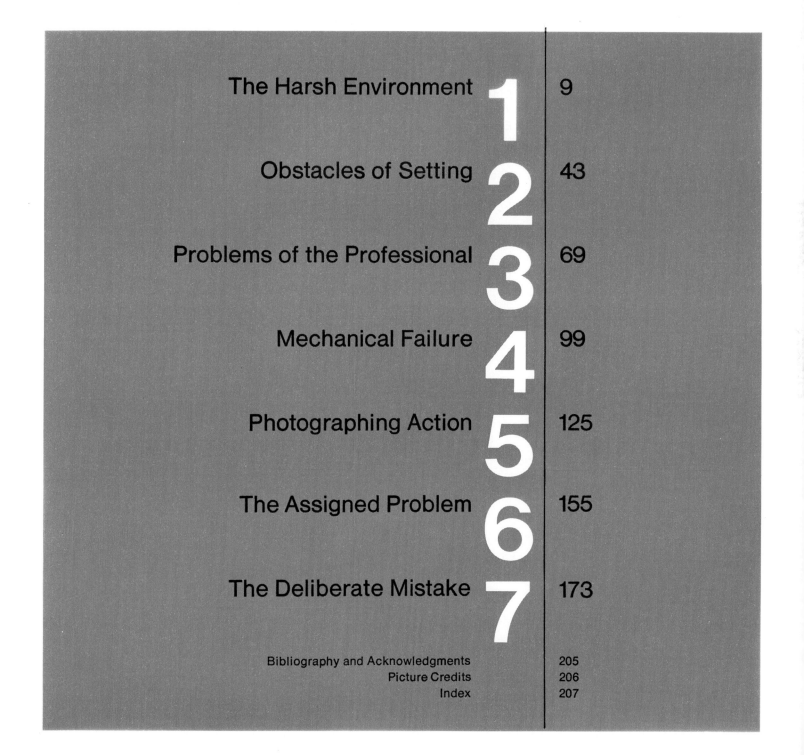

The Harsh Environment 1   9

Obstacles of Setting 2   43

Problems of the Professional 3   69

Mechanical Failure 4   99

Photographing Action 5   125

The Assigned Problem 6   155

The Deliberate Mistake 7   173

Bibliography and Acknowledgments   205
Picture Credits   206
Index   207

TIME-LIFE BOOKS

Founder: Henry R. Luce 1898-1967

Editor-in-Chief: Hedley Donovan
Chairman of the Board: Andrew Heiskell
President: James R. Shepley
Chairman, Executive Committee:
James A. Linen
Editorial Director: Louis Banks

Vice Chairman: Roy E. Larsen

Editor: Jerry Korn
Executive Editor: A. B. C. Whipple
Planning Director: Oliver E. Allen
Text Director: Martin Mann
Art Director: Sheldon Cotler
Chief of Research: Beatrice T. Dobie
Director of Photography: Melvin L. Scott
Associate Planning Director: Byron Dobell
Assistant Text Directors:
Ogden Tanner, Diana Hirsh
Assistant Art Director:
Arnold C. Holeywell
Assistant Chief of Research:
Martha T. Goolrick

Publisher: Joan D. Manley
General Manager: John D. McSweeney
Business Manager:
John Steven Maxwell
Sales Director: Carl G. Jaeger
Promotion Director:
Paul R. Stewart
Public Relations Director:
Nicholas Benton

LIFE LIBRARY OF PHOTOGRAPHY
Series Editor: Richard L. Williams

Editorial Staff for
Special Problems:
Editor: Robert G. Mason
Picture Editor: Patricia Maye
Text Editor: Jay Brennan
Designer: Raymond Ripper
Assistant Designer:
Herbert H. Quarmby
Staff Writers: George Constable,
Paula Pierce, Suzanne Seixas,
John von Hartz, Bryce S. Walker
Chief Researcher: Peggy Bushong
Researchers: Sondra Albert,
Kathleen Brandes, Malabar Brodeur,
Monica O. Horne, Myra Mangan,
Shirley Miller, Kathryn Ritchell
Art Assistant: Patricia Byrne

Editorial Production
Production Editor: Douglas B. Graham
Quality Director: Robert L. Young
Assistant: James J. Cox
Copy Staff: Rosalind Stubenberg,
Barbara Fairchild, Ruth Kelton,
Florence Keith
Picture Department: Dolores A. Littles,
Catherine Ireys

LIFE STAFF PHOTOGRAPHERS
Carlo Bavagnoli
Ralph Crane
John Dominis
Bill Eppridge
Henry Groskinsky
Yale Joel
John Loengard
Michael Mauney
Leonard McCombe
Vernon Merritt III
Ralph Morse
Carl Mydans
John Olson
Bill Ray
Co Rentmeester
Michael Rougier
John Shearer
George Silk
Grey Villet
Stan Wayman

Director of Photography:
Richard Pollard
TIME-LIFE Photo Lab Chief:
George Karas
Deputy Chief: Herbert Orth

Portions of this book were written by LIFE
photographer Mark Kauffman as well as by Photo
Equipment Supervisor Al Schneider. Valuable
assistance also was contributed by these
individuals and departments of Time Inc.: Editorial
Production, Norman Airey, Margaret T. Fischer;
Library, Peter Draz; Picture Collection, Doris
O'Neil; TIME-LIFE News Service, Murray J. Gart;
Correspondents Maria Vincenza Aloisi (Paris),
Margot Hapgood (London), Elisabeth
Kraemer (Bonn) and Ann Natanson (Rome).

The special problems of photography—and there are many—seldom discourage the serious photographer. On the contrary, these very problems stimulate his interest, their goad prodding him to some of his finest pictures. They excite him to stretch and extend the outer limits of his knowledge, and in the process acquire a better understanding of the full capacities of his camera, equipment and ingenuity.

The shot considered a routine assignment by an experienced professional may be a hazardous adventure for the beginner. But for photographers of every rank, certain special problems are universal. One is the all-pervasive power of nature's extremes; under the lash of a freezing rain or the heat of a summer sun, simply preserving film, lenses and camera—let alone getting a good picture—is a severe test. More exotic perils include the dust, fire and explosions of an erupting volcano or an insidious fungus that will spread over equipment in the damp tropics.

Mechanical failures that ruin a picture can be avoided by foresighted testing. But far more common are the problems of setting—reflections, obstacles, distances that get in the way of clear and dramatic pictures; yet all can be got around by the proper technique. There is one classic problem that has plagued and intrigued photographers since the development of the camera and can never finally be solved: how to convey a sense of action in the utterly motionless medium of still photography. But the attempts to resolve this problem lead to pictures that communicate the idea of action to the viewer.

These problems, while not those of every photographer, are basic to the entire photographic experience. To understand their traps is to begin to realize ways to avoid them. Or to make use of them. For some of the most exciting pictures are those that are deliberately shot the wrong way—and turn problems into advantages.

The Editors

The Harsh Environment 1

Perils of Heat and Cold, Dust and Dampness 12

The Challenge of Nature at Its Worst 26
A Volcano's Spectacular Hell-Fire 28
The Damp of Sea Air 30
Dust and Rain in the Tropics 32
The Spray of Pounding Surf 35
Dazzling Light, Frigid Cold at the Poles 36
Exploiting Antarctica's Brilliance 38
Antidotes for Sub-Zero Wind and Snow 40
Perils of the "White-Out" 42

BRADFORD WASHBURN· *Climbers in the snow at 11,500 feet, the Doldenhorn, Switzerland,* 1960

Perils of Heat and Cold, Dust and Dampness

In many ancient cultures, weather was thought to depend on the moods of the gods—and rather irascible gods at that. Fei Lien, the Chinese deity of wind, had a dragon's body and a powerful set of lungs that could blow up a typhoon in an instant. The Norsemen placed the blame for thunder and rain on Thor, a muscular redhead who wore an iron glove and wielded a red-hot hammer. Such notions may seem outmoded, but photographers in particular might be forgiven for continuing to suspect the gods of weather of occasional malevolence. For nature itself is often the culprit when pictures fail to come out. It is not the only source of trouble, of course. Setting and lighting pose their own problems, action is difficult to convey in a still picture, equipment goes on the fritz—and the photographer makes mistakes of his own. Yet the photographic obstacles presented by the natural environment are in many ways the trickiest to surmount.

Heat, humidity, rain, snow and cold all jeopardize photographic materials and equipment. Dust, sand and salt spray also bring their share of troubles, and even the unusual lighting conditions of a summertime beach or a snow-clad mountain can play hob with exposure calculations. The harm caused by environmental extremes may be immediately obvious. If the camera shutter does not work, the film-advance mechanism jams or the film snaps, the trouble is announced at once. But more often it is impossible to learn that something went wrong until later, when developed film turns out to be ruined or the effects of camera corrosion begin to show up.

In an era when people travel widely and routinely chronicle their journeys with their cameras, an understanding of the depredations of nature has become essential. As might be expected, the types of problems vary with the climate. Troubles encountered in California's Mojave Desert differ greatly from those that bedevil the photographer in Florida's Everglades. And the difficulties of the Massachusetts seacoast scarcely resemble those of the Colorado ski slopes. Yet none of the problems are insurmountable, and often they can be solved in very simple ways.

Heat is one of the most prevalent sources of photographic miseries. At the beach, in the desert, and in practically any locale where the sun's rays are intense, the camera's lens can be harmed if it is not kept sufficiently cool. When the air is 90°F.—a level that is still reasonably comfortable if the humidity remains low—direct sunshine may cause the dark, heat-absorbing body of a camera to rise to 120° or more. A camera that is stored in the glove compartment or trunk of a car may be even worse off, for temperatures there sometimes go as high as 150°.

Whenever the temperature of a camera exceeds 110°, trouble is possible —and sometimes it is disastrous. The lubricants in the camera can thin so much they run and gum up the delicate leaves that set the size of the aperture in the lens diaphragm. The cement that holds the glass elements of a lens together can soften and permit the elements to separate. And above 120°, bubbles could form in the optical cement, requiring expensive repairs.

To avoid such catastrophes on clear, hot days, keep equipment in the shade as much as possible. A leather case will go a long way toward shielding the camera and lenses from the sun's heat (professional photographers often carry their equipment in sturdy aluminum cases that reflect sunlight). However, a good protective device is also one of the simplest: a plastic picnic hamper, the inexpensive kind sold in hardware stores to keep food and drink hot or cold. Such hampers *(page 19)* offer satisfactory insulation from the sun's rays because their rigid plastic material is filled with air bubbles. They are also fairly strong and very light in weight.

Even these fine insulators have their limits, and the interior will heat up if the hamper is out in the sun for a long time, particularly after it has been

Despite the climate, Ralph Crane chose an outdoor setting for his portrait of Sheik Shakbut bin Sultan, ruler of Abu Dhabi, a small, parched sheikdom on the Persian Gulf, where temperatures routinely exceed 120°F. At the sheik's side is a $36,400, solid-gold model of an offshore oil derrick. It was presented by a grateful consortium of businessmen to whom Shakbut had granted an oil concession.

opened once or twice. One easy way to keep the temperature down under such circumstances is to keep a moistened towel on the hamper. LIFE photographer Ralph Crane chose another trick when he did a story on the oil-rich—and blazingly hot—kingdom of Abu Dhabi in 1963 *(preceding page):* each morning he placed a jarful of ice cubes in the Styrofoam hamper that he used to store his film and equipment.

An air-conditioned car is, of course, a great asset in hot climates—although, in rare instances, trouble may arise when equipment, cool from air-conditioned storage, is taken out into the broiling sun. The sudden heat starts all parts of the camera expanding, but since glass and metal expand at different rates, a lens may jam and make focusing impossible. LIFE photographer Henry Groskinsky ran into another sort of difficulty with air conditioning several summers ago when he was shooting pictures of houses in Houston, Texas, using large-format 4 x 5 and 5 x 7 cameras. He loaded the sheets of cut film into their holders while he was inside an air-conditioned house, then went outdoors to get some exterior shots. His mistake did not become evident until he developed the film and discovered that all his pictures were blurred. The cool film, subjected to a sudden rise in temperature, expanded so rapidly it buckled in the holders, throwing much of the image out of focus. This mishap could have been avoided by giving the film and holders time to warm slowly to the temperature of the surrounding air. (Such extreme buckling is much less likely with small-sized 35mm film.)

When high humidity is combined with heat, the problems worsen. In the swamps of Georgia or the bayous of Louisiana, the hostile alliance of these factors is at an extreme, yet a spell of muggy summer weather in Washington, D.C., may be troublesome too. The prime victim of hot, humid climates is film, especially after it has been unwrapped. Although modern film is very reliable and stable compared to that produced only a few decades ago, it still must be classed as a perishable product. This is hardly surprising, considering its make-up of organic gelatin (akin to gelatin foods used for desserts) and sensitive, microscopically small silver halide crystals that are easily triggered into changing their chemical form.

The combination of heat and humidity harms film in a number of ways. It can soften the gelatin so that developing solutions penetrate the emulsion at different rates when the film is processed. As a result, black-and-white pictures may seem unevenly exposed. Color pictures may appear washed out. And if color film's separate emulsion layers, which control the balance of color, are affected to different degrees, as is often the case in extremely humid tropical climates, pictures may have a reddish, bluish or greenish cast. In addition, extreme heat and humidity may act on the silver halide crystals just as light does, producing the unwanted overall exposure called fog. These types of damage can be inflicted either before or after the film has been exposed—although they do not show up until it is developed.

In hot, damp climates, film may also fall victim to fungus (sometimes called mildew or mold). Microscopic fungus spores are everywhere in the air, and given a suitably humid environment, they rapidly multiply on the film surface because its gelatin serves as food. After five or six weeks, they will produce visible splotches or cobweblike filaments on the emulsion. If the growth has not proceeded too far, the fungus can be removed from black-and-white film with special film-cleaning preparations, but color pictures may be hopelessly damaged, for the fungus releases substances that affect the color dyes. Fungus also attracts insects and bacteria that display a similarly voracious appetite for the gelatin. And over a period of three to six months, fungus can even grow on the lens, impairing light transmission and reducing the clarity of pictures.

Still another potential difficulty arises from the moisture-absorbing properties of film. In hot, damp weather the gelatin sops up humidity like a sponge, and when it becomes sufficiently swollen with moisture, the film may stick together in its cassette or on the take-up spool. If the photographer attempts to advance or rewind it, the emulsion side of the film may rip right off the film base, thoroughly ruining the pictures.

In any hot climate where the relative humidity remains above 60 per cent, film should be kept cool and (most important of all) dry, in order to avert loss of sensitivity, attacks by fungus and moisture absorption. One sound practice is to store the film in a refrigerator until it is to be used. However, this precaution will come to naught if the moisture-proof wrapping is removed the moment that the film is taken out of the refrigerator, for water droplets may be condensed out of the humid air by the chilled emulsion, causing spotting on the film. To prevent such condensation, the film should be left in its foil wrapping overnight so that it can warm up to the temperature of the surrounding air. In any case, it is best, in tropical climates, to load a camera during the daytime because the relative humidity is higher at night, making moisture condensation more likely then, even on film that is only slightly cooler than the air around it.

A second sound precaution is to keep film inside the camera for no more than a day or two so that it cannot swell up with moisture and stick together. This is particularly necessary on any extended field trip in a humid climate. For example, LIFE photographer Stan Wayman even went to the trouble of removing the film from his cameras every night when he was doing a story on fishing in Florida *(overleaf);* he qualifies as an expert on the problems of damp environments, for he grew up on a small farm in the Everglades. But

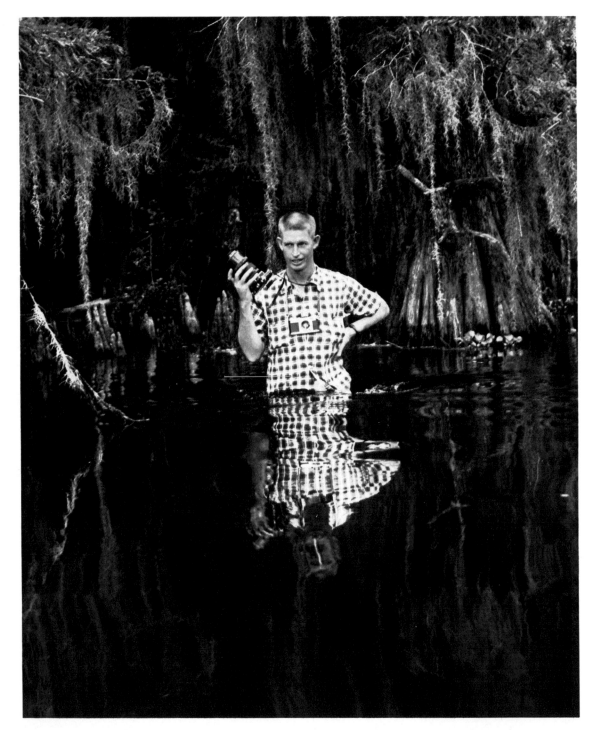

Hip-deep in a Florida waterway known as Fisheating Creek, Stan Wayman prepares to photograph an angler fly-casting for black bass. A specialist in outdoor subjects, Wayman has covered activities ranging from walrus hunts in the Bering Sea to scuba diving in Micronesia.

when an exposed roll of color film is removed from the camera outdoors, it should not be resealed in its original container until the photographer has reached some dry sanctuary, lest the humid outdoor air be locked up inside the can along with the film.

For travelers who will spend only a few days in a hot, damp climate, a convenient way to dry out exposed rolls of film—and keep them dry—is to place them in a suitcase containing freshly ironed clothes. Ironed linens absorb moisture well enough to hold humidity to a safe level. In the tropics, however, neither the suitcase nor the camera should be left in a hotel closet, for moth- and mildew-repellent compounds are often put there to protect clothes, and the vapor of these substances may react adversely with the dyes in color film. A slight amount of contaminated air may even remain in the camera long after it is taken from the hotel closet and even this trace of vapor is sufficient to continue to harm color film.

Much more reliable than ironed shirts as a defense against high humidity is a chemical drying agent, such as silica gel. Crystals of silica gel (white in their natural state but often treated with a bluish indicator dye) can keep the air in a small enclosed space as dry as Arizona. When the gel has collected all the moisture it can hold, the treated crystals turn reddish. But their humidity-countering powers can be revived by cooking them in an oven at 400° until they become bluish again. Silica gel is practically an ideal product: it is cheap; it can be reused indefinitely; and it is available at most photography supply stores, which sell it in small cans the size of shoe-polish tins, as well as in perforated plastic bags and bulk quantities.

On an extended trip in hot, wet climates, some photographers store equipment and exposed film with two or three perforated shoe-polish-can-sized containers of silica gel inside 10-gallon cans of the kind used for paint; their tight-sealing lids make them thoroughly moistureproof. A large, wide-mouthed glass or plastic jar with a vapor-tight cap will also serve as an excellent container for film and small items of equipment if silica gel is included. And even a Styrofoam picnic hamper, despite its lack of a tightly fitted lid, will usually remain sufficiently dry if it contains a liberal amount of fresh silica gel.

When silica gel is not available, ordinary rice can substitute as a drying agent, although about eight times as much will be needed. Before putting it in the hamper, first dry the rice over a low flame, then cool it in an airtight container so that it will not immediately absorb the moisture of the surrounding air. For convenient packets to hold rice or bulk quantities of silica gel in a hamper or equipment case, try ordinary socks; moisture is easily absorbed through the fabric of the socks, and there is no problem of loose grains or crystals scattering about.

Text continues on page 20

Choosing photographic gear for a trip is like packing clothes: the traveler should be prepared for many different situations, but not overburdened. The 35mm kit shown above can handle almost any situation an amateur is likely to run into. It includes three lenses: long, normal and wide-angle. A small electronic flash unit permits pictures in dim interiors. The plastic bags are useful to seal equipment and film against moisture or dust; but if very harsh conditions are anticipated, an underwater housing, costing $50 or so, is worthwhile.

1 | **lightweight tripod**
2 | **light meter**
3 | **spare batteries for meter**
4 | **film**
5 | **long lens and case (105mm for 35mm camera)**
6 | **normal lens and case (55mm for 35mm camera)**
7 | **wide-angle lens and case (35mm for 35mm camera)**
8 | **underwater housing**

9 | **35mm single-lens reflex camera**
10 | **leather neck strap**
11 | **polarizing, antiglare filter**
12 | **skylight filter**
13 | **haze filter**
14 | **lens hood**
15 | **camel's-hair brush**
16 | **electronic flash unit**

A trip to hot, damp regions calls for several additions (above) to the general-purpose gear shown at left. A foam plastic picnic hamper provides a cool container for equipment and film, and its temperature can be further lowered by packing it with refreezable units of liquid refrigerant. In direct sunlight moistened white towels thrown over the hamper help hold its interior temperature down. Towels can also be worn around the neck to keep perspiration off a camera. Other vital defenses against moisture include lint-free handkerchiefs for wiping the camera, silica gel desiccant to keep film dry, and an umbrella—the convenient, telescoping kind—for rainy weather. A metal neck strap is the best kind for carrying the camera, since leather straps may rot in hot, wet climates.

1 | **Styrofoam picnic hamper**
2 | **refreezable refrigerant**
3 | **umbrella**
4 | **metal neck strap**
5 | **silica gel drying agent**
6 | **lint-free handkerchiefs**
7 | **white towels**

In very cold climates, several extra accessories make it much easier to handle a chilled camera. Two pairs of gloves should be worn—a thick outer pair, and a thin inner pair that will enable the photographer to load or adjust his camera without directly touching the cold metal. The inner gloves shown above are made of aluminized fabric like that used for astronauts' spacesuits, but gloves made of silk, nylon or cotton will do. Since these thin gloves do not offer much protection against the cold, a hand warmer will be welcome after each loading session. Any metal parts of the camera that would touch the photographer's skin should be covered with the adhesive tape called gaffer tape. A stiff-bristled typewriter brush is an excellent aid for clearing snow from the camera's crevices. Light meters should be of the battery-less selenium-cell type, since batteries tend to lose their power in cold weather.

1 | **outer gloves**
2 | **inner gloves**
3 | **gaffer tape**
4 | **hand warmer**
5 | **typewriter brush**
6 | **selenium-cell light meter**

Far more troublesome than humidity, hot or cold, is water in any form—mist, rain, perspiration or ocean spray. When water gets inside a camera, it can rust metal parts, spot the film and cause other sorts of havoc such as shorting out the electrical circuit of the light meter. Perspiration is a worse offender than rain, for it contains salts and acids that quickly corrode metal. Prolonged exposure to salt spray is a foolproof recipe for rusting a camera.

In sweaty weather, many photographers wear towels around their necks so that perspiration does not drip into their cameras. Since hands will perspire, too, leaving salty moisture on camera surfaces, the camera should be wiped periodically with a lint-free cloth or chamois. Neck straps and camera cases made of leather are also prey to perspiration. Frequent waxing of the leather will help prevent rotting, but it is not a certain remedy in extremely damp climates. Co Rentmeester once went through seven neck straps in 10 days when he was shooting a story for LIFE on orangutans in Borneo *(right)*. The solution to the neck strap problem is simple: use a metal one.

In rainy weather some photographers wear a raincoat several sizes too large so that equipment can be comfortably carried underneath; but for all-around convenience, nothing beats an old-fashioned umbrella. However, it is no mean feat to hold an umbrella and shoot a picture at the same time, and occasionally the camera must be bared to the raindrops. A lens hood will usually keep the rain from getting on the lens and blurring the photograph. After the picture has been snapped, the camera should be dried out as soon as possible to prevent corrosion. Wiping it with a lint-free cloth will get rid of some of the water. Later, when the weather has cleared, the camera should be aired and then left out in the sun for a short time to exorcise the last of the moisture. A camera can also be dried in an oven for a few moments at a very low heat, but this procedure must be performed with caution.

Plastic bags—the self-sealing transparent ones used for food storage—provide very effective shields against rain or salt spray, and they are ideal containers for camera, lenses and film in a driving rainstorm, out on a boat or near the surf. It is even possible to keep a plastic bag over the camera while shooting. Just cut a hole in the bottom of the bag, making it large enough for the lens to peek through, then place a rubber band around the hole to clamp the bag to the lens and look through the open end of the bag to use the viewfinder for framing and focusing.

If a camera actually falls into salt water, it stands little chance of survival. Drying it out will not help. The only hope is to rinse it thoroughly, then keep it immersed in a pail of fresh water and get it to a camera repair shop as fast as possible. The immersion may seem suicidal, but it actually prevents air from reacting with moist salt and oxidizing the metal.

The ultimate in camera protection is afforded by a waterproof housing of

In the steamy atmosphere of a Borneo wildlife preserve, Co Rentmeester found an exceedingly friendly subject in one baby orangutan. Only about 4,000 of these primate relatives of man survive in the rain forests of Borneo and Sumatra.

the kind scuba divers use for taking pictures underwater. The housing consists of a rigid plastic box with a distortion-free glass front and attachments that enable the photographer to focus, advance the film and change exposure settings while the camera is sealed inside the box. (A housing that lacks these controls is considerably cheaper, but the camera has to be removed and reset after each shot.) Sealed in an underwater housing, a camera is totally watertight. It can be carried beneath the sea to a coral reef, plunged into a stream to photograph fish, or used for above-water situations that seem to be a prescription for disaster—such as standing close to a waterfall or leaning over the side of a sailboat to get a wave-level view of racing.

The main drawback of an underwater housing is its bulkiness. It is just not the sort of rig that lends itself to quick shooting or comfortable field work. If flexibility is essential and extremely wet conditions unavoidable, a better choice is an underwater camera such as a Nikonos, which looks like an ordinary camera but is totally waterproof.

Since wetness is so obviously harmful, logic suggests that photographic gear will be safe in very dry climates—but this is not the case, for dry weather usually means that dust or sand particles are floating or blowing about. Blowing dust and sand can etch the surface of a lens, gradually reducing its ability to give clear pictures. In addition, the fine, airborne particles penetrate the crevices of a camera. Once inside, they may jam the film-advance mechanism, slow down the shutter, or coat the inner surfaces of the lens so that light transmission is impaired. The dust may also get on the film, coating it with spots that block light and cause speckled pictures.

An indispensable safeguard for dusty regions is a clear or skylight filter kept over the lens at all times. Since these filters do not significantly affect the transmission of light from the subject, there is no need to calculate new exposure settings—and the filter shields the expensive lens against the direct assaults of flying particles. (Such filters are also very useful in wet environments to guard the lens against dried salt.) Dust and sand can be quickly blown or wiped away with a cloth or even the photographer's tie. The filter may not last long in a very dusty or sandy environment under such treatment, but a new one costs only a few dollars.

Not only the lens, but all other equipment needs protection from dust in dry regions. A coat or blanket can be thrown over photographic gear when it is not in use, but a case or plastic bag affords better protection. Despite the most meticulous precautions, however, some particles will probably find their way into a camera sooner or later, and the interior should always be checked before a new roll of film is loaded. Luckily, dust and sand are not particularly difficult to remove from a camera's innards. The simplest method is to blow them out by lung power—but there is always a danger that saliva will get into the camera. It is much safer to remove the offending particles with a sable or camel's-hair brush. A more effective device, available at most photography stores, is a rubber bulb that emits a stream of air when it is squeezed; on the opposite end of the bulb is a camel's-hair brush to clear away any particles that remain behind.

In very cold climates, the photographer has to run yet another gantlet of difficulties, which are often just as arduous as those encountered in hot, humid, wet or dusty environments. Shutters slow down, lenses ice over, exposure-calculations become mystifying, film snaps or is marred by electrostatic discharge, and the photographer himself runs the danger of frostbite from touching a freezing camera. However, several potential troubles can be eliminated by careful advance preparations.

One such problem is the slowing of a camera's shutter. Occasionally a chilled shutter does not operate as fast as the setting calls for, resulting in overexposure. In some cameras this lethargy is caused by the material used for their focal-plane shutters. It becomes so stiff and brittle at low temperatures that it resists movement; such cameras should be left at home. More often, the problem is due to thickening of the oil that lubricates the shutter mechanism. This happens less frequently nowadays because most new camera lubricants contain silicones, which do not become stiff until the temperature reaches −60°. Nevertheless, it is wise to check the camera before a winter trip to ski resorts or to northern Alaska. A convenient way of gauging cold-weather performance is to put the camera in the freezer compartment of a refrigerator for several hours, then take pictures at various shutter speeds. If any pictures come out overexposed, the camera should be handed over to a repair shop, where an expert will winterize it by removing most of the lubricants. (When the camera is brought back to a temperate climate, the lubricants have to be replaced to avoid wear and tear on the mechanism.) It is also good policy to have an expert make sure that a camera is perfectly light-tight. In snowy regions, where bright light is reflected from all directions, even a seemingly insignificant light leak can fog negatives.

Other hazards await as the camera becomes cold in the chill outdoors. One common mistake is to take warm equipment out into blowing snow. Snowflakes strike the camera, melt on contact and then refreeze. The only way to get the ice coating off is to take the camera back into the warm indoors. Yet this problem can be easily avoided by giving the camera time to cool down before taking it out of its protective case. When the metal surface is cold, snow that gets on it will not stick and can be shaken or brushed off.

Even after the camera has chilled to a low air temperature, freezing problems remain; they are simply different. For one thing, the lens ices up if the warm vapor of breath gets on it—as often happens when f-stop adjustments are being made. The moisture will instantly freeze when it touches the cold glass, but it can sometimes be removed by breathing on the lens again and then immediately wiping the remelted droplets off with a cotton cloth. More serious is the possibility that human skin will freeze to very cold camera surfaces. If a photographer puts his eye to an uncushioned viewfinder or tries to adjust the camera controls with his bare hands, his flesh may actually stick to the metal. To counter this hazard, tape sponge rubber, chamois or felt to the camera wherever it is likely to be touched. Another wise safeguard is thin silk or cotton gloves worn under the usual heavy gloves or mittens. The inner gloves not only keep hands warmer when the outer ones are removed, the thin ones make much easier—and safer—the loading and adjustment of a camera in sub-zero weather.

One almost certain casualty of cold is the cadmium-sulfide type of exposure meter—the kind built into most cameras. It operates on batteries, which not only lose power at low temperatures but are further drained by the heavy demands of the cell's reaction to the bright light of snowy regions. Spare batteries, carried in an inside pocket where body warmth maintains their strength, provide some insurance against meter failure. But a much better course of action is to use a selenium-cell meter, which has no batteries and hence is affected less by the cold.

Even with an accurate meter, there is a tendency to overexpose pictures in snow-covered terrain (as well as at the beach or in the desert), because reflectance of light is much higher than in an ordinary landscape. But if the picture includes a relatively dark subject—such as a person standing in the snow—underexposure rather than overexposure is likely. The strong light from the snow will distort the meter reading, and the person will come out dark and lacking in detail. To avoid underexposures, the meter should be held close to the person's face or clothes—or to the back of the photographer's hand, which has the same degree of reflectance. But the best course is extensive bracketing of all exposures.

A skylight filter is a useful aid to correct exposure in wintertime. It is almost colorless, but cuts down on the invisible ultraviolet light scattered by air molecules in the atmosphere; the reduction in ultraviolet helps prevent overexposure, darkens the sky in an attractive way, and also keeps the snow from appearing artificially blue in color pictures—an effect due to the reflection by snow crystals of the sky's ultraviolet, which registers as blue in color film. On the ski slopes, a skylight filter is indispensable because there is so much ultraviolet light at high altitudes that overexposure is very likely.

The film itself picks up peculiar ailments in extreme cold. Its sensitivity is not particularly affected, but it becomes very brittle. The edges of film hardened by the cold are so sharp that they can cut fingers during the loading operation. In the camera, the film must be advanced and rewound slowly or it will snap. When LIFE photographer Hank Walker was covering the Korean War in wintertime *(right),* his film often snapped because he advanced it too quickly during action-packed moments. He found that such mishaps could be greatly reduced by putting his cameras beneath his parka between shots; his body heat warmed the film and made it less brittle. Cautious movement of the film also avoids another cold-weather problem: electrostatic discharge. Moving film acts just like the rubbing surfaces in the electrostatic generators used for laboratory experiments; an electric voltage builds up on it, and a spark may actually leap from the film to the camera body, resulting in branchlike markings on pictures.

One final danger lurks at the end of the day's shooting in cold climates. If a chilled camera is taken back into the warm indoors, the moisture in the warmer air may condense on the lens, on the film and on the delicate inner mechanisms of the camera. The moisture may corrode the camera or spot the emulsion; and if the camera is taken back outside before the moisture has had time to evaporate, it will freeze solid and make picture taking impossible. The solution is to place the camera in an airtight plastic bag before going indoors. Moisture will condense harmlessly on the outside of the bag while the equipment inside warms up.

Some tactics apply to the problems of all climates. Certainly the first and most important rule does: keep the camera clean. Regularly use a cloth or camel's-hair brush to rid it of moisture, dirt or dust so that it does not fail at some crucial moment. It is bad enough to have picture quality slowly go downhill as camera performance deteriorates, but it is even worse to miss a great picture because the camera suddenly, without warning, refuses to work. Some camera failures that occur in the field can be remedied on the spot. The old trick of making a portable darkroom out of a coat, for example, may save the day when film jams after half a roll has been shot. The technique is simple: place the camera on the coat; button and fold the coat in such a manner that no light reaches the camera; reach backwards through the sleeves to open up the camera back; then free the film from the sprockets of the take-up spool and wind it back into its light-tight cassette. With the film thus rescued, the photographer can remove the coat and go to work on the camera to eliminate the source of trouble—perhaps a bit of sand or dirt that has gotten into the mechanism.

There are several other kinds of first-aid treatment for cameras. A small screwdriver often comes in handy to tighten up screws that have shaken

Hank Walker had to cope with temperatures that occasionally dipped to −30°F., while on assignment with an American patrol near the Yalu River (background) during the Korean War. In such extreme cold, film grows brittle. Film breakage was Walker's major problem.

loose during a trip across rough country. A roll of gaffer tape *(page 19)* is particularly useful. Tape helps to seal the crevices of a camera in very dusty regions. And if a camera has been accidentally dropped, bending the camera back so that light can penetrate it and fog the film, tape will provide a temporary seal until repairs are possible.

First aid will not always do the trick, of course, and the time may come when a photographer has to resign himself to the loss of a camera. To cover such an eventuality, professionals working with SLRs almost always carry a spare camera body (that is, a camera minus the lens). It provides an invaluable backstop and is not nearly so expensive as might be thought. The spare need not be an exact duplicate of the camera body ordinarily used. A less expensive model—perhaps lacking a self-timer or a very fast shutter—will be fine for back-up purposes, as long as it takes the same lenses the regular camera does. A secondhand body is generally good enough and may cost only half as much as a new one. But before starting out on a trip, have it checked out at a camera shop and then shoot a roll or two of film with it to compare its performance with that of the regular equipment.

The need for special gear and precautions to neutralize the hazards of nature may suggest that the camera should be left on the shelf at home except when the weatherman guarantees a perfect June day. Far from it. Most of the steps that safeguard equipment are simple. And some of the best pictures are obtained under the worst conditions. Photographers who surmount the problems of the environment find visual glories—the soft light and rich colors of rainy weather, the starkness of desert and plain, the translucent waters and dark tangle of the tropics, the fury of surf, the purity of snow. The difficulties are more than matched by the prize. □

The Challenge of Nature at Its Worst

Professional photographers have been engaged in an endurance contest with nature ever since their craft began, willingly accepting punishment of themselves and their equipment in an effort to get unusual pictures. More than a century ago, travelogue photographers ventured into the broiling heat and biting sand of the Sahara, across the snow of the Russian steppes, and up to the chilling winds of the Swiss Alps, bringing back exotic views that delighted a huge audience of stay-at-homes. Getting a good photograph under such climatic conditions was a difficult business at best. The collodion emulsion of wet plates—a predecessor of modern film—sometimes boiled in hot regions or hardened and became insensitive where the air was very dry. Countless pictures were spoiled when the emulsion picked up flying dust or when a drop of perspiration fell on the plate.

The invention of dry, roll film and rugged cameras has freed photographers from many of their former worries. But predictably enough, the professionals continue to reach for the outer limits of endurance. Today they tote their cameras to the South Pole where temperatures may sink to −100°F.; they defy the fury of hurricanes; they press close to erupting volcanoes; and they will undoubtedly follow the astronauts to the airless mountains of the moon if they can wangle transportation.

Like battle-wise soldiers, they have learned dozens of small ways to protect their gear. Thus armed, today's professional photographers have bested the worst that nature can present—and have brought back from their arduous campaigns such trophies of rare beauty as the ones on pages 27-42.

Heeding Death Valley's reputation for ▶ furnacelike heat—so intense at midday that the color balance of film might be affected—Charles Moore photographed the California desert between 5:30 and 7 in the morning, before the temperature rose above 80°. Even at that hour, the glare of the barren dunes required him to shoot at one or two f-stops smaller than the normal reading. A clear filter protected his lens from flying sand, but some tiny particles penetrated the crevices of his Nikon, and he had to clean out the camera later with a brush.

CHARLES MOORE: *Death Valley*, 1970

A Volcano's Spectacular Hell-Fire

ROBERT B. GOODMAN: *Fountains of Lava*, 1959

Despite its thrilling fireworks, the eruption of Kilauea Volcano in Hawaii seemed like a trial by torture to Robert B. Goodman, who photographed it for The National Geographic Magazine. The shaking earth blurred many of his exposures, and he used up a pocketful of lens tissues wiping pumice and rain off the protective filters over his lenses. He needed several cameras because grit continually penetrated and jammed them, even though they were wrapped with protective tape. When Goodman came close to the seething lava (right), the heat was so fierce that he had to focus and shoot in a few brief seconds, and then turn his back to recover. Of this assignment he later said, "Photographing a volcano is just about the most miserable thing you can do, but also the most fascinating."

ROBERT B. GOODMAN: *Lava Pool at Night,* 1959

The Damp of Sea Air

MICHAEL ROUGIER: *Fishing in Rajang River Delta, 1964*

A serene vision of a Borneo fisherman hauling up his nets at sunset belies the difficulties that Michael Rougier faced in this hot, humid climate. To ward off fungus, he carried his film in a picnic cooler lined with packets of the chemical dehumidifier, silica gel. After a day of shooting in the damp air, he used a portable hair dryer to get all moisture out of his camera.

JOHN DOMINIS: *Swamp in Dominica,* 1965

On the Caribbean island of Dominica, giant
pterocarpus trees hold within their gnarled
embrace an invisible threat to photographic
equipment—hot, damp air made salty by the
nearby sea. John Dominis minimized the
corrosive effect of this atmosphere by keeping
his camera in a strong plastic bag and removing
it just long enough to shoot the picture.

31

Dust and Rain in the Tropics

JOHN DOMINIS: *Oryx in Kenya,* 1969

Galloping across the parched grasslands of Kenya, a herd of oryx fills the air with fine, lingering dust. John Dominis turned the choking cloud to his advantage by positioning himself so that the sun was in front of him, backlighting the dust and producing a soft, luminous background almost like fog. He used a long 600mm lens and kept a considerable distance between himself and the skittish antelopes, but dust kept getting inside his camera anyway, and he had to clean it out every night with brushes and an air stream squeezed from a rubber bulb.

Water buffaloes and their youthful tenders calmly endure the whip of rain during monsoon season in Java. The downpour lasted only two minutes, but it proved costly to the photographer, Co Rentmeester. Although he carried an umbrella, wind-blown spray knocked his exposure meter out of action by causing a short circuit and also corroded his shutter so badly that he had to throw the camera away.

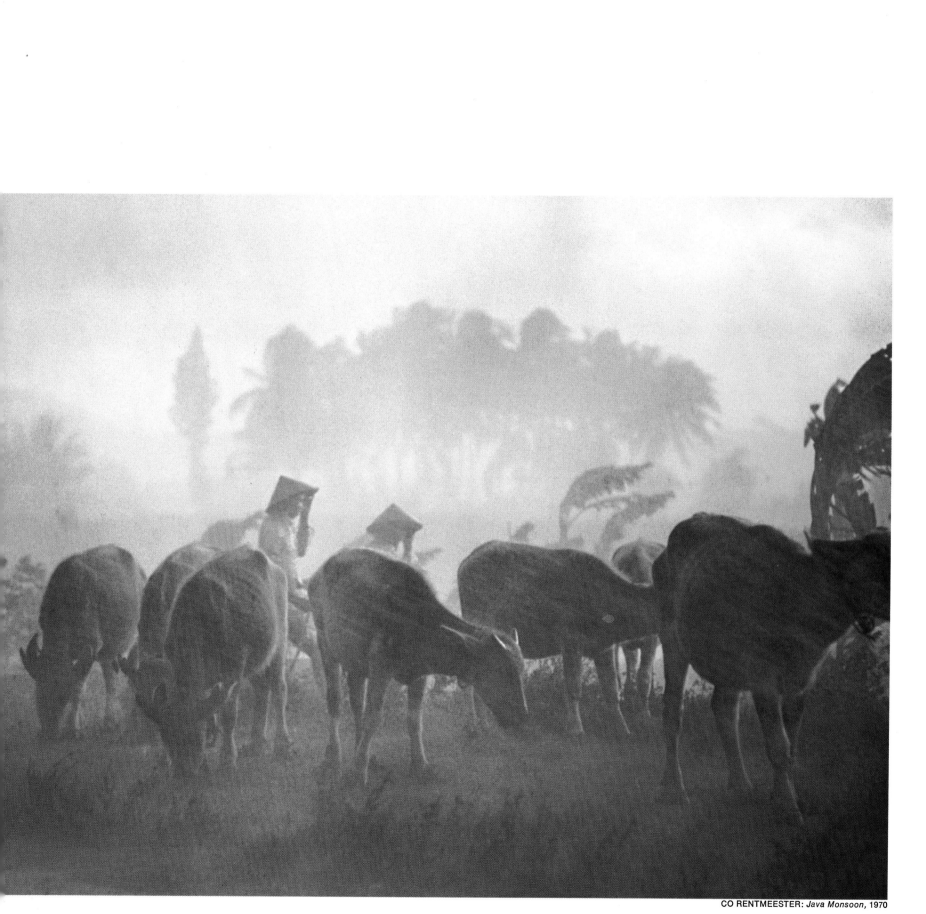

CO RENTMEESTER: *Java Monsoon*, 1970

LEONARD McCOMBE: *Storm Surf at Cape Ann*, 1962

34

The Spray of Pounding Surf

Storm-driven waves tear at the granite headland of Cape Ann, Massachusetts, as a lonely beacon in the background warns ships to stay clear. Leonard McCombe shot this picture of the sea's savagery an hour after sunset, using a tripod to steady his Nikon on the rocks. He protected his 200mm lens with a clear filter, wiping off spray just before he released the shutter. Then he quickly covered the camera with a plastic bag that kept out the corrosive spray.

Dazzling Light, Frigid Cold at the Poles

A whole new set of difficulties lies in wait for photographers who venture into the polar regions of the earth. Not only do low temperatures solidify camera lubricants and make film brittle enough to break if it is not advanced slowly, but the quality of the light is changed so much by snow and the low sun that exposure calculation is particularly demanding. Yet photographers travel to the Arctic and Antarctic in ever-greater numbers—for the simple reason that there is a surprising amount of activity there to be documented.

A million people live in Arctic lands, and unfamiliar species of birds and animals abound. Mining is a thriving industry in the frigid reaches of northern Canada. Tankers *(right)* and pipelines are thrusting into the icy Arctic realm to bring back oil from a pool underlying northern Alaska.

The Antarctic is an even more fearsome place. With an average altitude of 6,000 feet, it is the highest and coldest of all continents, its land and surrounding seas burdened with 90 per cent of the world's ice. Yet 10 nations have set up major camps in this lifeless, frozen land, for Antarctica holds important clues to global weather patterns, geological processes and the history of the planet. Photography plays an important role in all these scientific investigations, and also enables the world at large to see the work in progress. Even amateur photographers can now venture into this bleak region; one travel agency offers a tour of a United States camp that is perched in McMurdo Sound on the edge of the ice pack. □

Crunching through ice floes in the Arctic Ocean, the heavily reinforced tanker Manhattan nears the last leg of a voyage that tested the practicality of shipping oil from Alaska to the East Coast by a Northwest Passage. To get this picture from a viewpoint close to the ice-choked water, John Olson attached his Nikon to a 20-foot pole, held it over the side of the ship, and triggered the shutter with a cable release. He had already removed lubricants from the camera to prevent the shutter from slowing down or jamming in the severe cold. And before he went back indoors, he sealed the chilled camera inside a plastic bag so that moisture from the warm interior air would not condense on it.

JOHN OLSON: *S.S. Manhattan Heading for Alaska*, 1969

Exploiting Antarctica's Brilliance

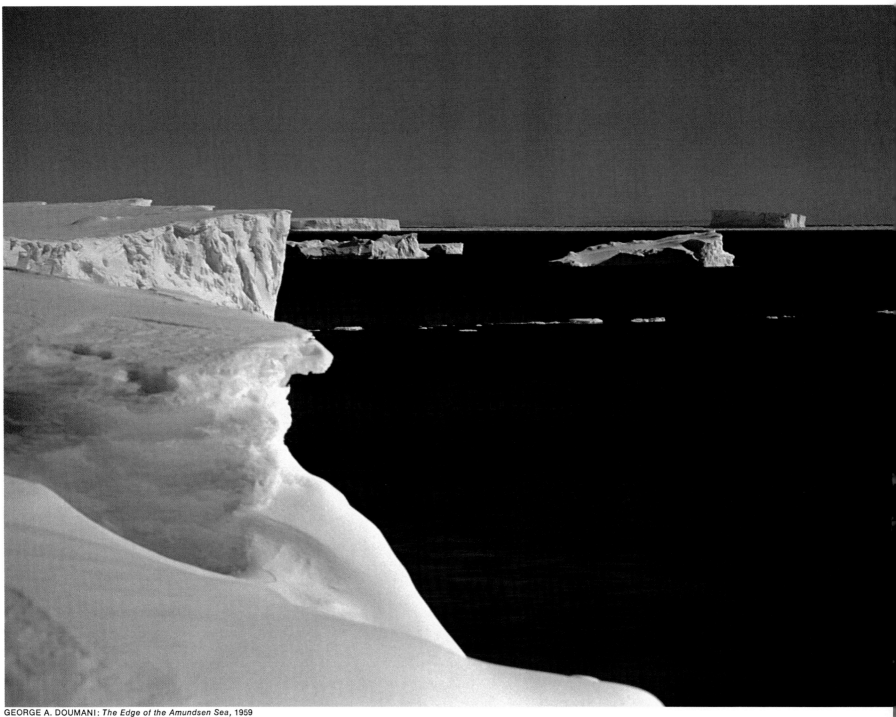

GEORGE A. DOUMANI: *The Edge of the Amundsen Sea*, 1959

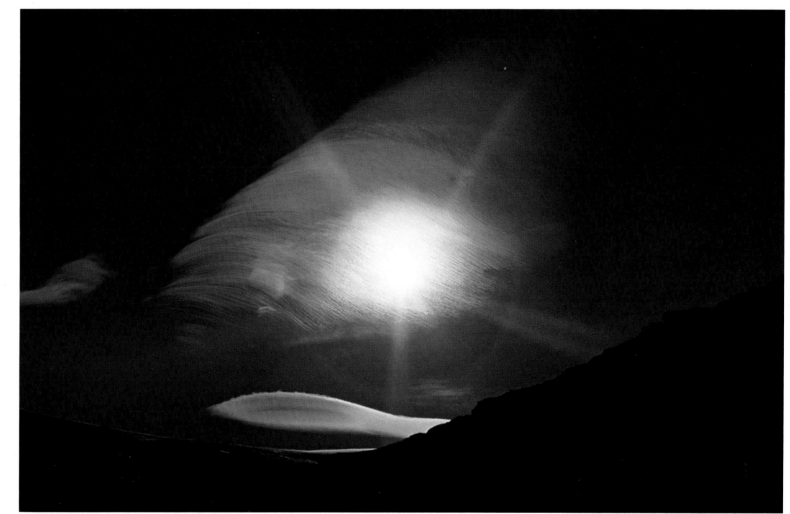

GEORGE A. DOUMANI: *Optical Effect of Clouds*, 1962

An ice shelf at the edge of Antarctica gleams gloriously white in the picture at left, taken by George A. Doumani, who is a geologist and glaciologist as well as a photographer. Using an ultraviolet filter over his lens, he blocked the great amount of ultraviolet radiation that the ice reflected from the sky, and thus reduced the bluish tinge such rays induce in color film. He also underexposed slightly to deepen the blue of the sea and show off the white ice to even greater advantage by heightening contrast.

To capture the unusual rainbow effect often observed around clouds laden with ice crystals, Doumani gauged exposure by pointing his meter directly at the Antarctic sun, then blocked the sun out of the camera's view by shooting from beneath a rock overhang. In effect, he was underexposing by several stops, thus suppressing the whiteness of the clouds and allowing the delicate rainbow colors to show up clearly. His meter was able to handle the direct rays of the sun because they were weakened by traveling a long distance through the atmosphere; in Antarctica, the sun never rises more than 50° above the horizon.

Antidotes for Sub-Zero Wind and Snow

Helicopters were grounded and scientists huddled inside their tents at Byrd Land Camp in western Antarctica when Navy photographer Robert R. Nunley ventured outside to take this chilling picture. The temperature stood at -30°F. and the wind was blowing fiercely. Under such conditions the slick metal of the camera would have instantly frozen to the skin of his face as he looked through the viewfinder of his Nikon, but Nunley averted this danger by covering up the metal with canvas tape. To keep the fine, blowing snow from penetrating the camera, he periodically cleaned the outer crevices with an ordinary typewriter-eraser brush.

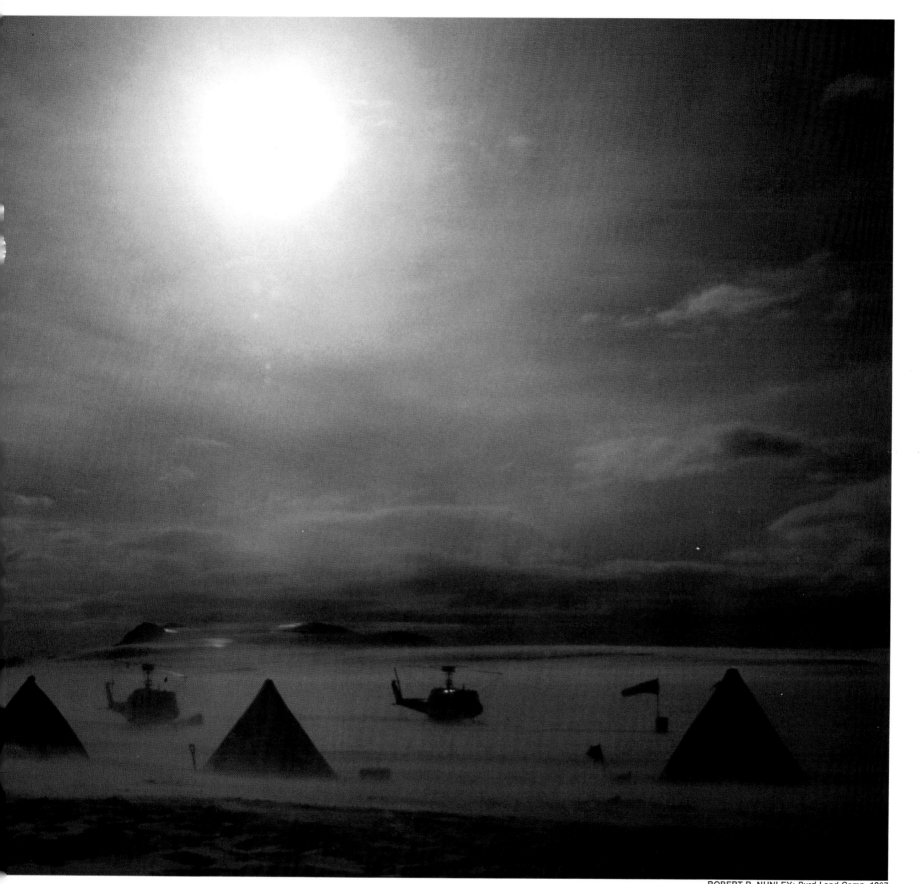

ROBERT R. NUNLEY: *Byrd Land Camp*, 1967

Perils of the "White-Out"

EMIL SCHULTHESS: *The Start of a White-Out,* 1958

A weary geologist, his beard caked with rime, returns from an expedition at the beginning of an Antarctic "white-out"—a perilous, disorienting condition when the reflection of light from the cloud cover and snow is almost exactly equal, and land and sky become indistinguishable. Focusing on the scientist's face with his winterized Leica, and shooting at 1/100 second and f/5.6, Emil Schulthess framed him against the rapidly disappearing horizon.

How to Get the Impossible Picture 46

Making the Foreground Disappear 48

Diffusing Distracting Backgrounds 50

Shooting Past Reflections 52

Shooting through the Looking Glass 54

Ducking Flare 56

Establishing Mood with an Enlarger 58

Far and Near in a Single View 60

Wide Angles, Distortion-Free, with a Special Lens and Camera 62

A Picture Lit by a Match 64

Adapting for High and Low Views 66

Making a Camera Shoot Sideways 68

Photographer Bob Walch looking through right-angle attachment (page 68)

45

How to Get the Impossible Picture

It is often said of problems that everybody has them—an undeniable but not very comforting sentiment. In photography, to be sure, one does not have to be a world-roaming adventurer to encounter difficulties. Problems lurk in the most everyday situations, where there are no glamorously extenuating circumstances, such as Amazonian heat or Antarctic chill, to help explain away a failure. Photographers constantly find themselves trying for interesting kinds of pictures, only to find that various difficulties undo their esthetic intentions. A scene shot through a window, or toward the sun, or into a mirror holds out the promise of special visual excitement, but the picture is very likely to turn out to be marred by distracting reflections, cascading splotches of light, or unexpected blurriness. If a photographer poses a person against a beautiful landscape and then steps close to get a good-sized portrait, the background may well be lost in a blur—and just knowing that it was there will make the picture seem all the more disappointing. Or a picture may fall short of its potential because the photographer didn't know how to deal with a background that was too busy, too bright, or the wrong color.

It is perhaps perversely logical that the most tempting pictures are frequently the hardest to get. Yet photographers need not accept this with a shrug, or rein in on their ambitions, for they have a great deal working in their favor. One of their biggest advantages in working with troublesome settings is mobility. By walking around a subject—a statue or a tree, say—a position can usually be found where distracting backgrounds, unwanted shadows, or flare-inducing lights are eliminated. Shots taken from a kneeling position will silhouette the subject against the clear, neutral background of the sky. A bird's-eye view may give an inkling of the subject's general environment —for instance, locating the statue in a tiled courtyard or the tree on a lawn —while holding back other details of the surroundings in a tantalizing way. And if the subject is mobile too, any setting can be maneuvered into submission, for the photographer will not have to give up a particular angle of view in exchange for ridding the scene of some obstacle.

The camera itself provides all sorts of means for dealing with troublesome surroundings. The most important are the familiar options of aperture size, shutter speed and focal length of the lens. Consider, for instance, the problem of taking a portrait in a city street, a setting with plentiful variety and vitality. In the mind's eye of the photographer, the person in front of his camera is an attention-drawing presence, and he expects the camera to render the subject that way. But the anticipated center of interest may not materialize in the photograph. The person may appear diminished and anonymous in a welter of signs, passing cars and hurrying bodies. Yet these distractions might have been easily nullified. The photographer could have found a quieter backdrop by walking around his subject or posing the person in a carefully chosen spot. He could have set the camera diaphragm at a wide aperture, reducing depth of field and blurring the background. He could have selected a slow shutter speed so that the cars and passersby would turn out blurred while his motionless subject remained sharp (provided that the camera was braced against a wall or car to prevent shake). Or he could have taken the picture with a long lens whose narrow angle of view would catch only a small segment of the bothersome background.

This is not to say that a bustling, dynamic background should be divorced from a portrait on grounds of incompatibility. The urban setting may say something quite revealing about the person who is being portrayed, in which case the photographer may want to pursue wholly different tactics—freezing the intricate motions of the city with a fast shutter, extending the depth of field with a small aperture, and perhaps pulling in a generous sweep of view with a wide-angle lens.

A number of specialized camera accessories are available to help cope with difficult settings. Polarizing filters will cut down on reflections; red or yellow filters will enable a camera to peer through mist by blocking the blue and ultraviolet light scattered by water droplets; there is even a split filter —one half red-tinted glass and the other half clear glass—that is designed to darken a sky and bring out the whiteness of the clouds while leaving the lower half of a landscape unaffected so that no detail will be lost. A somewhat similar device, resembling a simple lens cut in half, allows a camera to focus at two different distances at the same time—one possible solution to the problem of getting a background and a foreground both in focus.

Equipment manufacturers are pressing toward a state of affairs where no situation could be said to be impossible. They offer periscopelike lens attachments for shooting to one side or around a corner; they make lenses that can scoop in a very wide-angle view with scarcely any distortion. Even almost total darkness—the ultimate obstacle in photography—has been conquered. Photographers today can employ a device called a low-light-camera system *(pages 64-65),* which multiplies the intensity of light so dramatically that a short-exposure picture can be taken by starlight.

Making the Foreground Disappear

The grizzly bear resting in New York's Central Park Zoo is in sharp focus but can hardly be seen through the bars and mesh shielding his den. Freelance photographer Paul Jensen made this picture as a demonstration, using a small enough aperture—f/11—to provide sufficient depth of field to keep both the foreground cage and the background bear sharp.

Many a potentially interesting photograph is ruined because of distracting obstacles cluttering the foreground. A photographer standing at a window and trying for unself-conscious pictures of children playing in the street may find his view is obscured by the window screen. Such sports events as tennis matches take place in areas enclosed in mesh fences. And animals like the grizzly bear above are most easily found behind the bars of a zoo cage.

Such barriers can be wiped out of the picture by simple focusing changes. If the obstacles are sufficiently blurred, they will not show. A long-focal-length lens, which has restricted depth of field at short distances, makes it easier to throw foreground subjects out of focus. But even with a normal lens, much of the heaviest foreground obstruction magically melts into an almost invisible blur when the aperture is opened wide, or when the photographer moves in close to the obstacle, and focus is adjusted for the distant subject.

In some cases the photographer may wish to retain a sense of place or to make a point by keeping in his picture a soft suggestion of the foreground obstacles. For instance, he might want to show the hazy leaves of the blind in which he hid to photograph wildlife, or show the bars of a circus cage to emphasize that the lion tamer is right inside with the dangerous animals.

In the picture above, Jensen maintained his focus on the bear, but decreased his depth of field by opening the aperture to f/2.8; he also moved up close to the fence. The links of the cage have practically disappeared, and the thick iron bars, now dim and blurred, are all that remain to show that the bear is caged. Even the bars could be cropped from an enlargement.

Diffusing Distracting Backgrounds

When a busy background spoils a normal composition, there are two simple means of dealing with the difficulty. First, the background can be thrown out of focus by decreasing depth of field until only the subject itself is sharp, clearly delineated in the foreground. A long-focal-length lens, because of its severely restricted depth of field, when used to photograph objects near at hand can help to blur a distracting background, but simply increasing the aperture without changing lenses will have a similar effect.

Second, the photographer can shift position to change the angle of his shot, so placing himself that he can picture his subject against a less cluttered background. On a busy city street, he might move to a point where the background consists solely of a blank wall; in the countryside he can avoid the distraction of a background tree by turning to set his subject against an open field. Choosing a high angle, so that the background is plain ground or pavement is another stratagem. But a common dodge is simply to drop to one knee, shoot from a low angle and silhouette the subject against the sky —the technique that freelance photographer George Haling finally used to obtain the picture he wanted *(opposite, far right)* of a New York traffic sign.

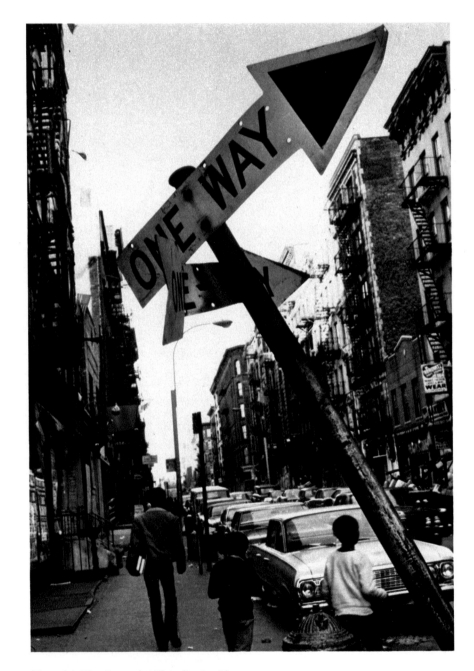

Sharp detail far down a bustling city street is caught in this picture shot at f/32, an extremely small aperture that gives great depth of field. But so clear a background distracts the viewer from the subject: a sadly smitten traffic sign.

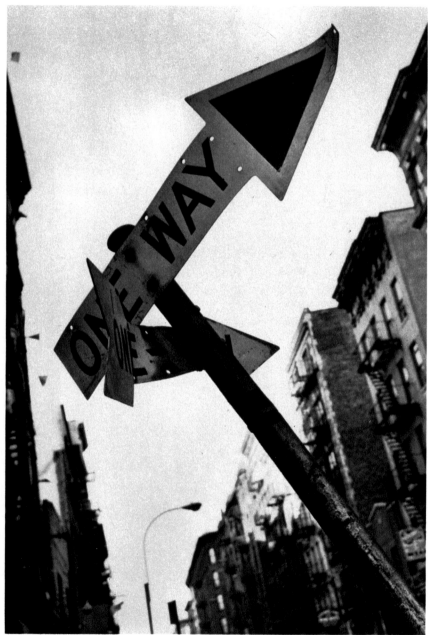

When the lens was opened to f/4, depth of field was so reduced that even the parked car a few feet away from the battered sign was thrown out of focus, and the design formed by its tormented arrows is sharp in comparison.

Changing the angle and shooting upward made the sign's outline stand out as the background virtually disappears. The buildings, fairly sharp at a moderate aperture, approximately f/12.5, now serve only to frame the sign against the sky.

Shooting Past Reflections

Freelance Bob Walch dextrously manipulated a polarizing filter to control the reflections that make nonsense of the picture at left above. He eliminated just enough reflection in the picture to the right to clear up the lettering inside the window, the condensed steam running down it and the smiling child, still leaving the dim image of the buildings to maintain a sense of place.

There are various ways to overcome the distraction of surface reflections when photographing an object behind a pane of glass. One of the best methods depends on the fact that all reflections from any such nonmetallic surface as glass consist of polarized light —light rays that vibrate only in one plane. The reflection can thus be reduced by a polarizing fiiter, which

blocks off the rays in a single plane of light. It is easy to swivel the filter around until the plane it blocks coincides with the plane of the reflected rays, thus trapping the reflections while leaving the subject clear in the viewer. When taking a picture through a window, a polarizing filter is most efficient if held at an angle of about 35° to the surface, because it is at that angle that maximum polarization occurs. In order to compensate for the light lost in the blocked rays, open the aperture 1⅓ stops wider than the meter reading.

Without a polarizing filter, the most obvious technique is to move around until obtrusive reflections are at a minimum. But this works only when the camera angle is unimportant, and even this technique will not always work —especially on bright days. Another method, mainly good for small subjects behind the glass of a window or showcase, is to move close to the glass —even to the point of touching the front of the lens housing to the glass— so that the photographer and camera shield the window, preventing the formation of reflections that the camera can catch (above).

In the first shot (above left) the crystal bonbonnière in a display window is barely discernible beyond dazzling reflections from the street. By moving in close to the plate glass (right), the photographer screened out the reflected car and buildings, while the covered candy dish, as seen in this cropped enlargement, still gleamed with its own reflections, lit from angles he had not blocked.

Shooting through the Looking Glass

The first thing to keep in mind when photographing an object and its reflection in a mirror is the optical law that light from an image in a mirror has to make a double journey: it must travel from object to mirror, then from mirror to eye or film. This doubles the apparent distance between the reflection and the object being reflected, raising focusing difficulties when both are to be included in the picture *(right).*

Depth of field is again the factor that controls success with such pictures. Changing to a lens of shorter focal length gives greater depth of field, but may introduce size distortions, particularly in close-ups.

Retaining the normal lens but stopping down its aperture is a simpler way to increase depth of field and is often sufficient, provided allowance is made for the range of sharp focus. At distances of less than five feet, focus the camera midway between reflection and real object. At medium distances—5 to 15 feet—focus on a point about a third of the apparent distance between the two. Such a focus makes the most of the available range of sharpness.

The three pictures at right and opposite of a bouquet in front of a mirror show the traps of shooting an object with its reflection—and how to avoid them. All three photographs were taken in natural light, from a sunny window, with a Leicaflex, using a zoom lens set at 90mm. In the first two shots (right and center) a wide aperture, f/5.6, so restricted depth of field that when the camera was focused on the bouquet, the mirror image appeared as a misty blur, and when the focus was set for the reflection, the flowers were blurred. Decreasing the aperture to f/16 enlarged the depth of field, and carefully adjusting the focus—bringing it closer to the foreground than the background—made all parts of the scene come out sharp (far right).

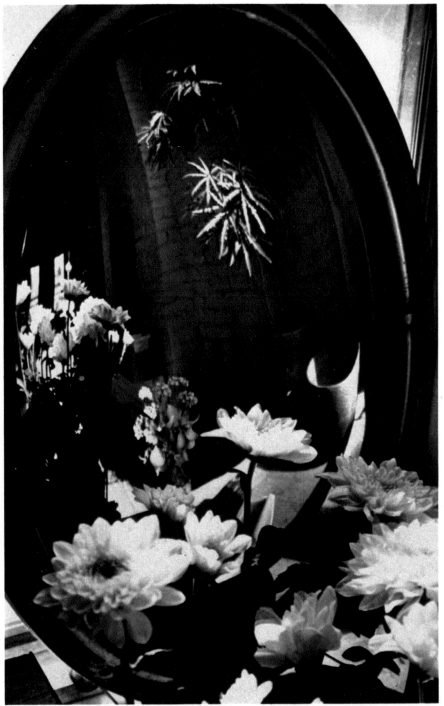

Ducking Flare

Flare—a loose term denoting bright spots on a picture caused by light reflections on the surface of a lens, inside lens elements or in the camera body itself—is normally avoided by obeying a hoary bit of advice: do not shoot directly into the sun or any other light source. This advice is not always easy to follow, and sometimes following it will not solve the problem. If, for example, a photographer is shooting a seaside scene, brilliant light will enter his lens from a variety of sources—from reflections off the water, from the white sand, perhaps from the metal parts of beach gear, as well as from the direct rays of sunlight angling in—any or all of these sources can produce flare spots in the finished picture.

A light source can cause flare even when it is out of the field of view of the picture—oblique rays are bent into the camera by front surfaces of the lens. The wider the aperture the more opportunity for such unsuspected light to enter and to spread. Thus, the photographer who is shooting under conditions in which he suspects flare may occur should use a lens hood, and stop down for as small an aperture as possible. Alternatively, he may solve the problem by changing his position, placing the object he wishes between lens and light source—the simple trick that was successfully employed to take the picture on the opposite page.

Shot into the sun, this attempt to portray the stark outlines of a telephone pole resulted in a classic example of "iris flare." Sunlight entering from the side bounced around the elements of the lens and generated multiple reflections of the hexagonal shape of the open diaphragm of the Nikon F used to take the picture.

With the camera moved to a position behind the subject, so that it blocked the direct rays of the sun, the photographer was able to shoot toward the light source and still avoid flare—and get the picture he set out to produce.

Establishing Mood with an Enlarger

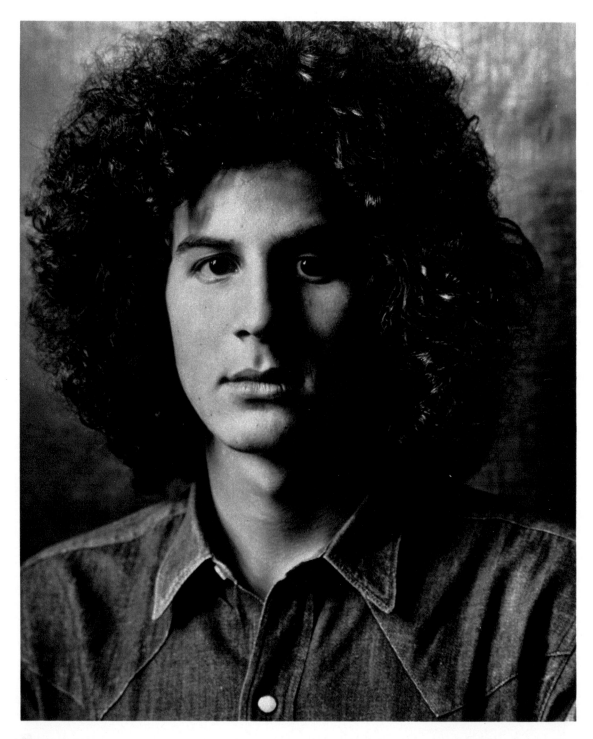

Some problems in photography can be solved simply by switching from one type of enlarger to another. In pictures, and particularly in portraits, that rely on such subtleties as shading or detail, mood can be significantly altered by the type of enlarger used in printing. Such a contrast shows up in the pictures on these pages. Both prints were made from the same negative; the one at left with a condenser enlarger, the one opposite with a diffusion enlarger.

The diffusion enlarger has a light-dispersing system, usually a milky glass plate between negative and lamp, that is designed to spread light so that it continues to spread slightly after passing through the negative. Since the light rays are diffused when they reach the enlarging paper, details are softened and tones muted. For portraits, such prints are often pleasing because the lack of sharp definition and crisp shadows can be flattering. But some of the light is lost when it passes through the glass plate, requiring an increase in exposure time.

The condenser system is more efficient. Working on the same principle as a spotlight, a pair of condenser lenses focuses light so that the light rays do not spread, making sharp prints with bold contrasts and tones. Where the finest detail is to be rendered, the condenser enlarger is generally the choice.

Made with the intense, focused light of a condenser enlarger, this print is sharp in its contrast and tones. The lighting and highlights are bright, the shadows very dark in the areas under the chin, creating a harsh quality. The brilliance of the light in the enlarger also brings out vividly the texture and sheen of the shirt.

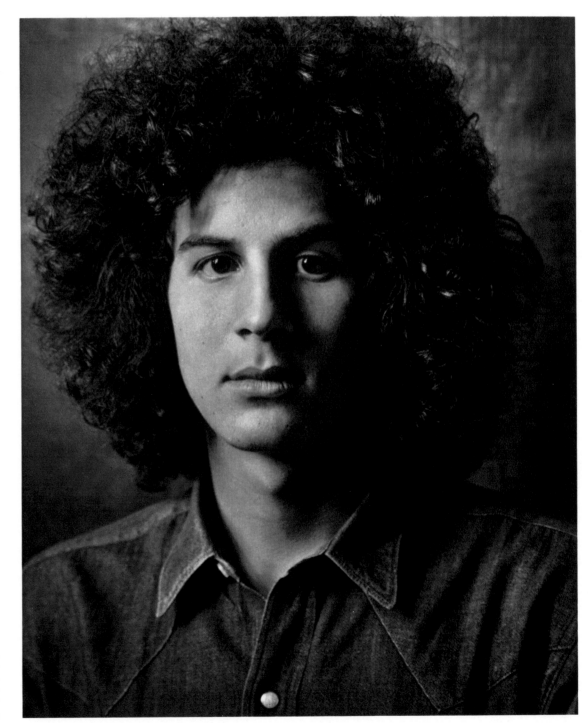

Made from the same negative as the picture opposite, this print shows the gentler tones created by a diffusion enlarger. Well-suited for portraits, the diffusion enlarger softens shadows and facial markings. The shirt texture has receded as a factor in the portrait and the mood of the shot is one of peaceful tranquillity.

Far and Near in a Single View

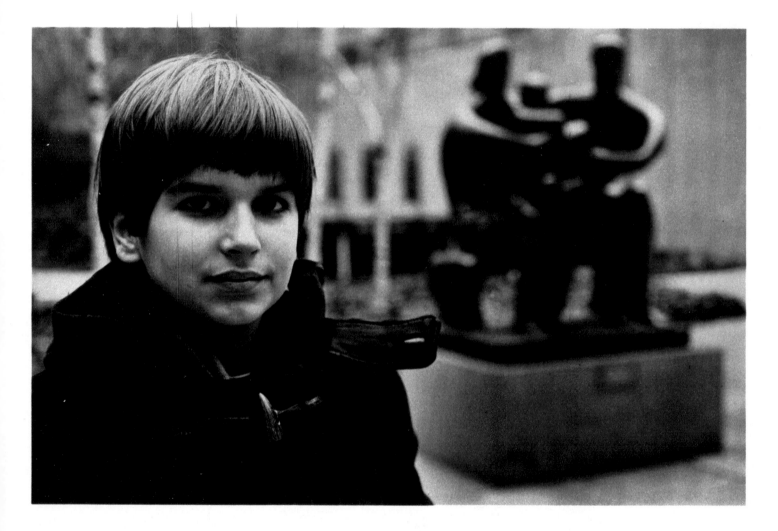

The outdoor portrait above was taken on an overcast, blustery afternoon in the sculpture garden of New York's Museum of Modern Art with a normal lens set at f/5.6 and focused on the boy, who was standing about four feet away. The sculpture in the background, less than 20 feet away, is reduced to a blur. Forced to focus on the foreground, even the smallest aperture on the lens could not have made both parts of that picture sharp.

Getting an outdoor portrait that preserves the sense of setting provided by sharp background details is difficult because the usual means of increasing depth of field cannot always be used. Even a very small aperture does not give sufficient background sharpness when the subject is close to the camera. And a wide-angle lens, for all its great depth of field, is no help because of the distortion it creates in nearby objects. To capture both the near and far

without distortion, the lens must focus on two distances at once. This can be done with a split-field close-up lens —one half is a supplementary lens that puts nearby objects in focus, while the other half is either plain, flat glass or simply empty. This half-lens, mounted as shown opposite, alters the focus in half the view, enabling the photographer to keep his subject sharp in that half while the background remains sharp in the other, unaffected half.

To get the clear images above, the photographer placed the split-field close-up attachment (right) over one side of his lens. He focused on the sculpture in the unaltered right half of the scene. He then had the boy move forward and back until his image, seen through the close-up side, was also in focus. That the lens-plus-attachment actually focused on two different planes at once is revealed by the birch trees in the background, which are blurred to the left of center but sharp to the right.

Wide Angles, Distortion-Free, with a Special Lens and Camera

The "barrel distortion" flaw found in many extreme-wide-angle lenses on 35mm cameras—it makes horizontal and vertical lines bend in at the picture edges *(above)*—is eliminated by using an unusual lens whose design was cranked out with the aid of an electronic computer by Zeiss designers Fritz Köber and Erhard Glatzel. It provides a 15mm lens, the Hologon, that covers a 110° angle of view with practically no distortion *(opposite),* bending light rays uniformly no matter how far from the center of the scene they originate.

For this wide-angle uniformity, the designers of the Hologon lens had to allow for some strange characteristics. The rear lens element is so thick and sharply curved that it must be positioned less than ⅕ inch from the film, and the only camera the lens will fit is one made specially for it, the Ultrawide.

The middle of the lens—where an adjustable diaphragm normally goes—is completely taken up by the center element. So there is no diaphragm; the lens is built to provide an aperture of f/8, and exposure is varied only by changing shutter speed or film. There is no focusing adjustment either, because the great depth of field keeps everything in the photograph sharp from 20 inches to infinity.

◄ <u>Not</u> only the Salvation Army musicians but the skyscrapers surrounding them in the narrow Channel Gardens (opposite) of New York's Rockefeller Center can be brought into one 35mm picture by an 18mm lens—its very short focal length covers an angle of view of 148°. But in doing so, it must bend light rays from the edges of the scene more than those from the center, and straight lines seem to curve inward.

The picture above covers 110°—close to the angle of view shown opposite—but with scarcely any distortion. Only the man at the extreme right seems oddly stretched. This shot was made with the 15mm Hologon lens in the Ultrawide camera (right), which is so designed that the disproportionate bending of light rays from the edges is canceled out in the lens. Like most wide-angle lenses, however, it provides less illumination at the edges than in the center. The nonuniform exposure has little effect on black-and-white film; for color the effect can be compensated by a graduated neutral density filter whose density becomes progressively greater toward the center.

A Picture Lit by a Match

Even when the only light available is the flare of a match, it is still possible to get a clear picture with a low-light-level camera system *(below)*, made by Singer Librascope. Using techniques originally developed for the United States forces in Vietnam, it has been used for night surveillance there and for police stakeouts across the country.

The heart of this complicated device is an image-intensifier tube. Its front end is a light-sensitive surface, somewhat like the one in a television camera tube, that converts the light energy into electrons. Its rear end is a screen that converts electrons back into light. In between are amplifying circuits to make the light generated at the rear 7,500 times stronger than the light coming in at the front.

The system employs two intensifiers working in sequence behind a lens with a very long focal length—300mm or 500mm. The image on the rearmost screen is relayed by a second lens system to an ordinary 35mm camera. The combined light gathering power of all this apparatus is equivalent to an aperture of f/.2; the light has been magnified more than 10,000 times, enough to make visible people 400 feet away on a moonless night. Its cost: about $8,000.

In the low-light-level system, which is 25 inches long and weighs 25 pounds, the largest section is the light-collecting lens. At center is the electronic gear that amplifies the light, while the adjoining relay lens passes it to the camera.

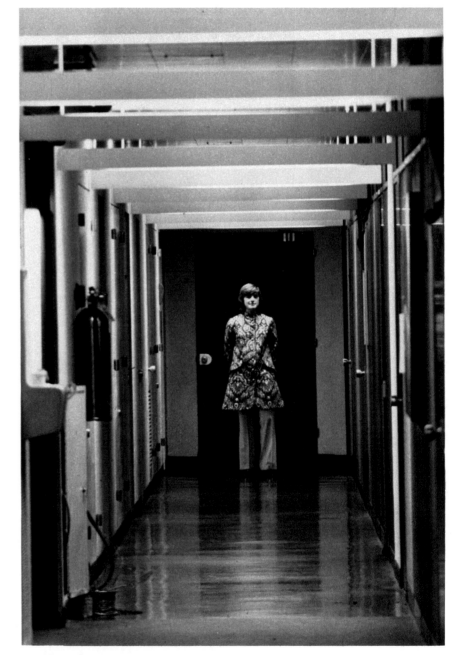

To take this picture with a standard Nikon with a 300mm f/4.5 lens, every light in the corridor had to be turned on for the two-second exposure. In all three pictures shown here the girl was 168 feet from the camera and the film was ASA 400.

Using the low-light-level system attached to a 35mm camera, the girl is photographed at 1/30 second with every light in the corridor off. The only illumination is the beam from a flashlight shining on the girl from a nearby doorway.

Only the lighted match the girl holds aloft illuminated this picture also taken at 1/30 second with the low-light-level camera system. Every other light source was extinguished; even the glass above the doors was blacked out.

Adapting for High and Low Views

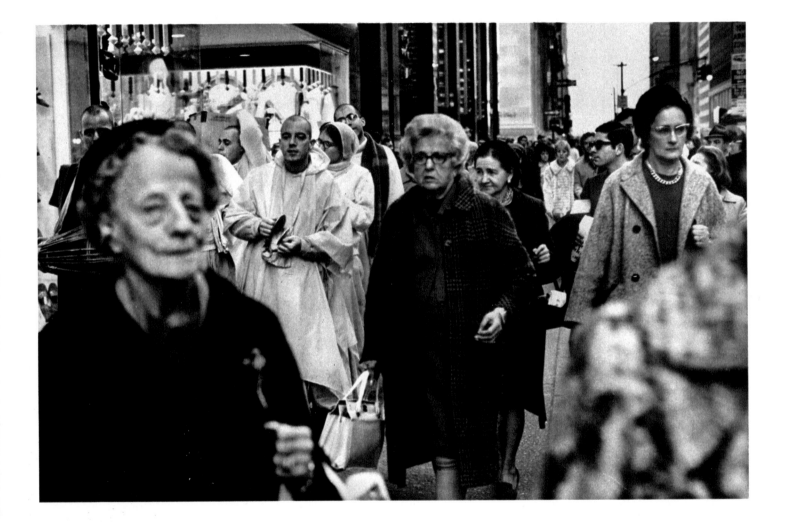

When shooting in a crowd—whether at a sporting event, at a parade or merely on a busy street—the photographer often finds himself unable to get an unobstructed view of his subject. A vantage point above the activity is the ideal solution, but it is not always available. In that case, there is another option: the photographer can simply hold his camera up at arm's length and shoot over the heads of the crowd.

Certain cameras lend themselves to this procedure because of their viewing systems. Thus, although a photographer working with a rangefinder camera can only aim in the general direction of his subject and shoot blind in such a situation, he is at no disadvantage if he has a twin-lens reflex: its ground-glass viewer enables him to hold the camera overhead, upside down, and see the picture he is taking. Most single-lens-reflex cameras can be easily adapted to work in much the same way. On some of these cameras, the ground-glass focusing screen remains locked in place when the prism is removed and can be used as a viewer just like that on a twin-lens reflex. On other SLRs, the prism and ground glass come off together. In that case, a special attachment called a waist-level viewer—simply a ground glass with pop-up metal sides which serve as light shields *(opposite)*—can be slipped into place to serve the same purpose.

In the photograph opposite, the exotic group of ascetics at left is nearly lost among the more ordinary passersby. The photographer could not halt the pedestrians in order to shoot the group alone. To compose and focus the clear view above, he put on the accessory waist-level viewer shown at right, which made the viewing screen visible with the camera held an arm's length away. He moved out to the curb to avoid being jostled, raised his camera overhead, then looked up into the ground glass to see—and shoot—over the intervening crowd.

Making a Camera Shoot Sideways

People who suddenly discover that they are being photographed almost always freeze up—and the opportunity for a natural picture is lost. One way around this problem is a device *(below)* that enables the photographer to take a picture of a person to one side of him while he aims a camera straight ahead. The attachment has a false glass front so that it appears to be merely an extension of the lens. But inside the barrel is a mirror placed at a 45° angle to turn the field of view to one side. With an easy rotation of the attachment, the photographer can also see up or down —all while his lens seems to be pointed at other subjects. ☐

Believing the camera is not trained on them, the people at right are at their most natural. The attachment that catches them this way is the spiratone Circo-Mirrotach, made to be attached to long-focal-length lenses (100mm or longer), primarily on single-lens-reflex cameras (above). The Circo-Mirrotach picks up images through a mirror that enables the photographer to shoot down (top) or sideways (bottom), but which reverses right and left in the picture.

Problems of the Professional 3

A Gadgeteer's Exploits 72

The Experts' Ingenuity 82

A Ghostly View of a Live Concert 84

Switching Ordinary Equipment to Special Tasks 86

Totaling Up a Teacher's Workday 88

A Polite Way to Make People Vanish 90

"Profit by My Mistakes" 92

The newly completed Time & Life Building in mid-Manhattan seems to burst skyward like a song of pure technology (opposite), yet the picture was taken with aged, jury-rigged equipment. Yale Joel used a 75-year-old view camera with an extreme wide-angle lens, and held it out over the corner of the building with a 15-foot pole. The shutter was designed to be tripped by air pressure from a rubber bulb, but the bulb could not transmit enough pressure at that distance—and so he replaced it with an ordinary bicycle pump. While Joel (foreground, right) supervised the aiming of the camera, an assistant, at the base of the pole, operated the pump and snapped this arresting view.

YALE JOEL: *Time & Life Building*, 1961

A Gadgeteer's Exploits

On the following pages, Al Schneider, head of the Equipment Section of the LIFE Photo Lab, discusses some of the special gear that he has built to solve photographers' problems. Beginning on page 92, LIFE photographer Mark Kauffman recounts some of the harrowing—but instructive—moments of his career:

Photographers continue to startle me with their requests for special rigs to make some kind of unusual picture. They have asked the Photo Equipment Department to build everything from lighting equipment that would illuminate an entire stadium—for a panoramic view of a football game at night—to a sparkproofed camera that, without any remote controls, would automatically photograph astronauts just as they entered their space capsule. Usually the solution to the problem turns out to be so simple it's almost funny; when Yale Joel asked for a compressed-air supply to work the shutter of a camera dangling from a boom [*preceding page*], a bicycle pump filled the bill. And then there is the $1.75 switch that makes stunning photographs of motion; it depicts action in two different ways in a single photograph—providing the blurred effect of a time-exposure as well as the motion-arresting effect of strobe.

Joe Scherschel raised that problem. He had been assigned to cover the beginnings of commercial Boeing 707 flights at Kennedy Airport in New York. He wanted to get a picture of the plane as it took off at night, and he could not decide between a stop-action picture with strobe and a time exposure that would show the streaks of the jet's lights. As he talked, it became clear that the best picture would show both views.

The solution was a common kind of switch having a very long name: a double-pole double-throw momentary contact switch with an OFF position in the center. Set one way, it could feed power to the camera; set the other way it could feed power to a strobe [*diagram opposite, bottom right*]. Joe took the picture [*opposite, left*] with a view camera whose shutter was tripped by a solenoid—an electromagnet that pushed a piston against the shutter button. The shutter was set on BULB so that it would stay open as long as the piston pushed. When he threw the switch into its forward position, electric current activated the solenoid and held the shutter open, so that the film recorded time-exposure streaks from the lights of the plane. When he threw the switch into its back position, the strobe was fired. At the same time, the solenoid circuit was broken, allowing the shutter to close—but not before the strobe-lit jet registered on the film. In fact, the view camera's large, leaf-type shutter closed so slowly that it was still partly open after the flash died out, and, in the picture, streaks of the plane's lights continue on past the strobe image. The editors of LIFE liked this effect and ran the photograph. But nowadays, for this technique, we use a camera with a fast-closing focal-plane shutter,

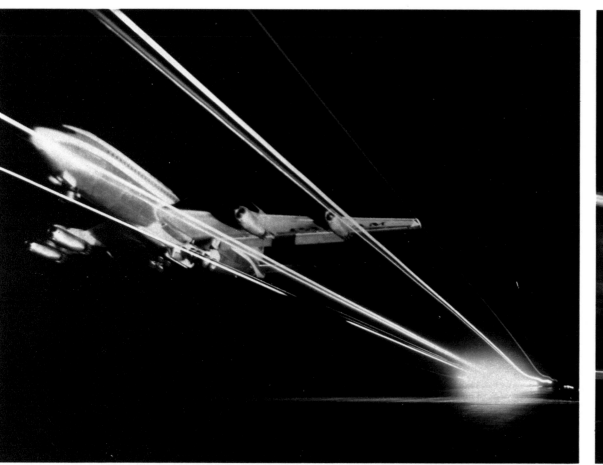

JOE SCHERSCHEL: *Climbing 707*, 1958

TONY TRIOLO: *Off the Springboard*, 1963

double-pole double-throw switch

The "double-pole double-throw momentary contact" switch at left is designed to create two versions of motion in a single photograph —time-exposure streaks or blurs, and a sharp, motion-freezing image. As diagramed at right, it controls both an electrically operated camera and a strobe unit. As long as its handle is turned to connect the terminals to its left, the switch holds a camera's shutter open; when flicked past the center (OFF) position over to the right-hand terminals, it stops holding the shutter open and fires an action-stopping strobe just before the shutter has had time to close. In the picture of the jet airliner above, the streaks from the landing lights continue on past the strobe image because the leaf-type shutter of the view camera closed slowly. A camera with a fast-closing focal-plane shutter was used for the picture of the jackknifing girl, so that the strobe image was the very last thing that the film registered.

motorized camera

double-pole double-throw switch

strobe unit

73

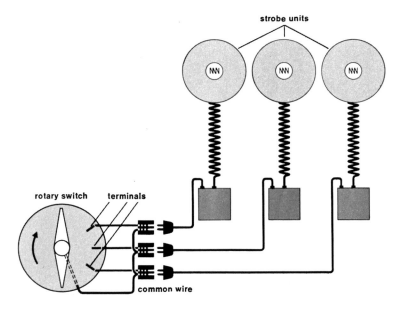

so that the blurred time-exposure portion of the picture comes to an abrupt end as soon as the strobe is fired [*preceding page, right*].

Many of the gadgets that we have built over the years are intended to give photographers more flexibility with lights, particularly strobe. Often there is a need for a strobe that flashes repeatedly to produce multiple images of a golfer's swing or a ballet dancer's leap in a single picture. Some strobes are specially designed to work that way—but they are bulky, heavy and very expensive. And while they give out enough light for good black-and-white pictures, they often are not powerful enough for color. On the other hand, regular strobe units give out plenty of light, but can seldom fire at a rapid rate. The answer to the problem is a switching system that triggers a whole battery of ordinary, powerful strobes one after the other. The device that we came up with does the switching electronically; it has no moving parts—just vacuum tubes, capacitors and so forth. Ten strobe units can be plugged into it, and they can be triggered sequentially at any rate from one flash every second to 12 per second.

The electronic sequence switch is easy to control, and it fires the strobes at very regular intervals. But if perfect spacing of the flashes is not essential, a manual system can operate strobes in sequence. Several strobe units—of any size—can be controlled with a gadget called a single-pole rotary switch, which can be bought at any radio supply store for about $2.00. Wires from the individual strobe units are attached to the terminals of the switch [*diagram, right*] and the lights are fired off in rapid succession when the rotary switch is given a quick twist by hand.

Sometimes photographers want to create a sense of motion where there is none. In principle, this is a cinch: just pan the camera while the shutter is open. But it's not so easy to pan a camera smoothly and at an even rate. Getting a really good illusion of motion requires a tripod with a motor-driven head. And this was exactly the equipment that Yale Joel requested some years ago when he wanted to use the panning technique to get some out-of-the-ordinary pictures of motorcycles. I told him that a motorized tripod would be very expensive, since it had to be especially machined and geared. Joel nodded understandingly and disappeared.

A few days later he showed up with the necessary equipment—an ungainly rig that he had put together with a few dollars' worth of old parts [*diagram, opposite page*]. He had dug up an old sewing machine motor from somewhere and fixed it so it would turn a belt that slowly rotated a tripod head. It looked like a real Rube Goldberg contraption, but it worked like a charm.

To get one photograph, Joel brought a motorcycle to the studio and had a model sit on it. He told her to lean forward as if she were roaring along a road, but of course she wasn't going anywhere. (In fact, the motorcycle was

Several strobe units can be fired in rapid sequence if they are wired into an ordinary rotary switch as diagramed above. A common wire connects one half of each strobe circuit to the movable part of the switch. The other half of each strobe circuit goes to a separate terminal on the switch. The photographer simply twists the switch, and as it turns it completes one circuit after another, firing one strobe after another to produce multiple images of a moving subject. Any number of lights can be used: the switch box below, used by LIFE photographers, can handle 17 strobe units (the camera sync wiring plugs into the eighteenth socket).

switch box

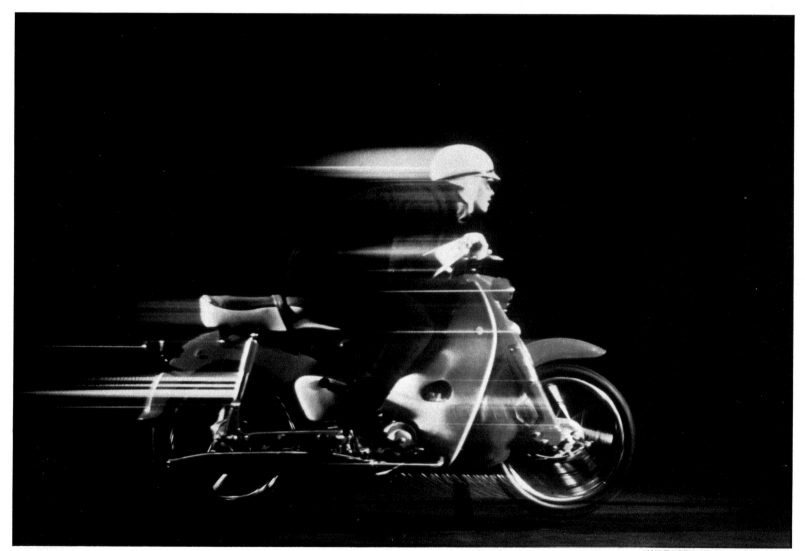

YALE JOEL: *Illusion of Speed*, 1965

floodlight

tripod head

flash unit

camera

rheostat

pulley belt

sewing-machine motor

rheostat

The girl who seems to be racing along on her motorcycle in the picture above was not actually moving—but the camera was. Yale Joel used the rig diagramed at left to get the photograph. A rheostat, connected to the sewing-machine motor, allowed him to control its speed as it turned the tripod head on which his camera was mounted. The camera was pointed behind the motorcycle when he began the time exposure. When the panning camera was aimed right at the girl, he dimmed the floodlight with a second rheostat, fired a flash bulb for a bright stop-action image, and closed the shutter.

resting on its parking stand—although that did not show when the picture was printed in LIFE.) Then he went to work. First he switched on his motor. The camera, which had been aimed to one side of the girl, slowly panned toward her. He opened the shutter, and it stayed open because it was set on BULB, producing a blur of illusory movement on the film. Just when the camera was pointed straight at the model, Joel dimmed the lights, set off a flash bulb and immediately closed the shutter. The bright flash registered the girl's image strongly on the film and froze her motion—which was really the camera's motion. The nicest touch of the picture is the whirling of the motorcycle's front wheel. Since the parking stand lifted the front wheel off the ground, Joel was able to give it a good spin for verisimilitude before he began his complicated exposure.

Only slightly less strange-looking than Joel's sewing-machine-motor contraption was an essential piece of equipment improvised to cover rocket launchings at Cape Kennedy. The National Aeronautics and Space Administration has a rule—a necessary one—that any electrically operated camera or switch in the launch area must be completely sealed in a container filled with nitrogen gas. Unlike air, nitrogen does not support combustion, ensuring that an electrical spark will not set fire to the volatile rocket fuel. But, of course, a nitrogen-filled container for a camera would be very expensive if it had to be designed and built from scratch—which is what NASA had done for its own cameras. We found a short-cut. We took a clear plastic camera housing, ordinarily used for underwater photography, and equipped it with intake and exhaust valves so that air could be pumped out and nitrogen gas could be pumped in [*right*]. Perhaps it isn't the most beautiful article of equipment in the world, but it is perfectly airtight and safe.

We used a similar, slightly larger housing for the launch of the Apollo 11 moon rocket in 1969. The editors had asked for photographs of astronauts Armstrong, Aldrin and Collins just as they were entering the capsule on top of the rocket. After months of negotiation and paperwork, NASA reluctantly gave permission to mount a nitrogen-filled housing along the steel walkway that led from the gantry tower to the capsule. However, for safety reasons, no wire or radio remote control could be set up to operate the motorized camera, so a NASA technician was enlisted to switch it on when the astronauts approached the walkway. But there was another problem. Armstrong and Aldrin were scheduled to enter the capsule first; five minutes later, after they were buckled into their seats, Collins would arrive. This meant that if the technician threw the switch and started the camera snapping pictures of the first two astronauts at the rate of two per second, all the film would be gone by the time Collins arrived.

Once again, there was a simple solution: a small, motor-driven timer. It

Because of the danger of a spark setting fire to the highly flammable rocket fuels at Cape Kennedy, all electrically operated cameras covering a space launch must be enclosed in a nitrogen atmosphere, which will not support combustion. Rather than design and build a brand-new housing for their camera, the LIFE Photo Lab adapted a plexiglass housing formerly used for underwater photography, on the sensible assumption that if it kept water out, it would keep gas in. Two valves were inserted in the side of the housing so that air could be exhausted and nitrogen pumped in. The cylinder at the front of the housing is a heavy-duty battery to drive the 250-exposure motorized Nikon. The circular bolt at the upper left-hand corner is used for mounting the camera housing.

microswitch

arm

adjustable timing wheel

motorized camera

automatic three-camera timer

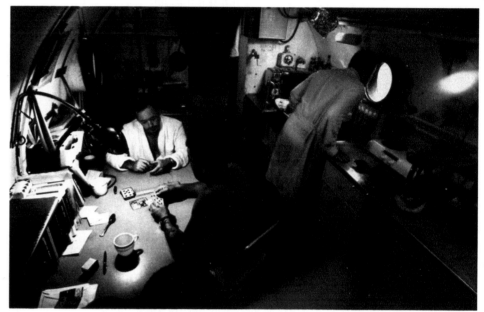

The timer shown here is driven by a continuously operating electric motor and can automatically trigger a motorized camera at regular intervals, minutes or hours apart. Essentially the timer consists of a small switch whose arm is pressed against a steadily turning wheel (diagram, top). When the arm of the switch dips into a notch on the revolving wheel, two contacts in the switch close, and electrical current flows in the circuit that operates the camera. The wheel is really two similarly shaped disks—called cams —sandwiched together. By manually rotating one of the cams while keeping the other still, the width of the notch can be adjusted, changing the length of time that the camera will shoot. The frequency at which the camera shoots depends upon the preset speed of the revolving cams. The timer shown in the photograph directly above has three sets of wheels and switches, enabling it to control three cameras. Ralph Morse employed it to regulate the photographic coverage of the activities of aquanauts in Sealab I (at right, above), a submergible Navy research vessel constructed to explore the problems of living under water for extended periods.

was installed in the housing along with the camera and programmed to fit the circumstances. As soon as the technician threw the switch, the timer went into action. Its electric-clock motor turned a cam that closed a circuit and started the camera shooting rapidly. After a few seconds, the timer switched the camera off; then five minutes later it switched it on again—exactly when Armstrong started to cross the walkway—and the camera shot the rest of the roll. Luckily for us, astronauts are very punctual.

Timers, even simple, inexpensive ones, are very useful in photography. When a motorized camera is set for continuous shooting, the timer can start or stop the shooting at predetermined intervals, as one did for the moon-launch pictures. If the camera is set for single shots, the timer can trip the shutter for individual pictures at almost any rate; for example, to get a time-lapse sequence of pictures showing a flower bursting into bloom, a motorized camera can be set in position and connected to a timer that will trigger it every few minutes, completely automatically. There are dozens of timers on the market, as a glance at any electronics supply catalogue will show. They range from the kind often used to turn house lights on and off to deter burglars, some of which cost less than $10, to very expensive ones meant to control complicated manufacturing processes. Our timers cost about $30 each, and one of their advantages is that they can regulate several independent operations at once. Ralph Morse called on this ability when he was doing a story on Sealab I in 1964.

Sealab I was a submergible structure that was lowered 192 feet below the surface of the ocean off Bermuda. The United States Navy had built it for a research program to see if men could live and work under water. Morse was not allowed to go down with the aquanauts; nor could he operate the cameras by remote control, since there was no electric-wire contact with the surface, and radios do not work under water. So he substituted a timer for himself. He mounted three motorized cameras inside Sealab—one trained on the hatchway, one on the working area and one on the bunkroom. The aquanauts were instructed to switch a camera on whenever they entered a particular area and switch it off when they left, in order to save film. Once started, each camera automatically proceeded to shoot at its own distinct pace, because the cameras were wired to the timer, which had three separate cams [*preceding page*] to trigger each camera at a different rate. When the hatchway camera was turned on, it took a picture every 10 minutes, the workroom camera one every 20 minutes, and the bunkroom camera one about every hour. As it turned out, his carefully orchestrated sequences did a fine job of documenting the activities of the aquanauts.

That assignment might have been muffed if Morse had not remembered one small detail. The atmosphere inside Sealab I was at a much higher pressure than that at sea level. It was so high that it might have caused the cameras' lens elements to implode, because the airtight lens barrels contained air at ordinary pressure. This disaster was averted by drilling tiny holes in the lens barrels, permitting pressure inside and outside to be equalized as Sealab was lowered into the depths.

Not all problems can be solved so simply, however. When strobe flash units first came into wide use in the 1950s, for instance, there was no way to trigger the lights without being tied to them by electric wires. The "sync cord," which sets off the strobe when the shutter is tripped, was often a bother. To cover a big dance, a photographer had to string sync cords between his camera and the strobes mounted around the ballroom. The wire linkage usually took a couple of days to set up, and it restricted the photographer's movements when he was shooting. So, in 1955, we set out to replace the wire with radio. Two units were needed—a transmitter, plugged into the camera and carried by the photographer, and a receiver that was plugged into the lights. When the photographer tripped the shutter, the radio transmitter would send a signal to the receiver, instantaneously setting off the strobes. We hired an electronics specialist to help us design and build the system [*right*]—a process that took two long years. Sometimes the radio receiver that triggered the lights was set off by electrical interference from water coolers or cash registers. But when all the bugs were worked out, the radio linkage gave LIFE photographers a tremendous advantage in covering large

transmitter transmitter receiver

receiver

motorized camera

new system

original LIFE system

The original LIFE radio system, a pioneering tool for remote control of strobe lights or a motorized camera (above, right), has been supplemented by a more compact system, as the side-by-side comparison above suggests. The old transmitter and receiver together weigh 15 pounds and have a maximum range of one-and-a-half miles. The new, commercially available radio system weighs a total of three-and-a-half pounds and permits remote control from as far as three miles away. Made by Jacobson Photographic Instruments of California, it can transmit and receive signals on five different channels—a valuable feature if there are other transmitters in the vicinity.

interior scenes like political conventions or basketball games. (Today, of course, similar gear, factory made, is widely used.)

The radio remote control proved very useful outdoors, too. When the receiver was attached to a motorized camera instead of to lights, the photographer could take pictures from a mile or more away just by pressing a button on the transmitter. In fact, one of the first jobs for the radio system was at a sports car race in Wisconsin. Joe Scherschel mounted a camera on the hood of one of the cars and operated it by radio from a hillside where he could see the whole race. Action pictures like that had been taken before by having the driver operate the camera with a cable release—but at tense moments in the race, when drama was at a peak, the driver usually had other things on his mind than tripping a shutter.

But an attempt to use radio control in a similar situation almost ended in disaster. Jerry Cooke wanted to shoot a new kind of picture of a harness race for SPORTS ILLUSTRATED. Since a horse pulls a sulky in a harness race —instead of carrying a jockey in the saddle—there was an obvious opportunity to use radio remote control. The track officials reluctantly gave permission to mount a motorized camera and radio receiver on a sulky, facing backwards to show the trailing drivers and horses as they went around the course. The officials were nervous about the idea because these were real races with a lot of money at stake, and thousands of bettors were going to be very angry if the equipment affected the outcome.

Well, Jerry Cooke is a very calm guy, impossible to fluster. As one race got under way, we were standing in the infield of the track, and he was watching through binoculars and operating the transmitter to get photographs of the action. I heard him say, "Okay, they're going around the curve . . . they're bunching up very nicely . . . we're getting some good pictures . . . oh my God, the camera is falling off." All in the same calm tone of voice. I had visions of disaster if the equipment fell into the path of the horses behind, and maybe some violent mob action after that. But we were saved by the skin of our teeth. I had wrapped a piece of baling wire around the body of the camera just as a precaution. It held, and the sulky finished the race with the camera dangling behind.

LIFE photographers still use wires for remote control of their motorized cameras where radio is prohibited. In fact, the "direct-wire" system can be given a lot more flexibility by building a gadget that allows the wire between the photographer and camera to be very long. Normally, a motorized camera is operated from a distance by pressing a button on a battery pack, which then sends electricity to run the camera motor. In most cases, the wire from the battery to the camera should be no longer than about 500 feet; beyond this length, the losses in the wire will weaken the current so much that the camera motor will not function. But there is a way around this difficulty: use two batteries. One is placed with the camera, and the other with the photographer. The battery attached to the camera runs the motor and is turned on and off by a relay, an electrically operated switch [*right*]. The signal activating the relay comes from the battery near the photographer, and since the relay needs only a very weak signal to work it, the photographer and the second battery can be as far as two miles away. This is a pretty substantial improvement, considering the relay costs only about $15.

Recently, Ralph Morse employed this system at Fort Sill, Oklahoma, for a story on an unusual junk-disposal technique. The Army is doing its bit to clean up our environment by using junked cars for target practice at its artillery range. While the artillerymen learn accuracy, the old cars are blown to smithereens by the exploding shells. Morse wanted to place his three cameras fairly close to the cars to get dramatic views of their destruction, but he could not go into the target area, of course. Nor could he use radio to operate the cameras, for the Army had so many radios in the vicinity that they interfered with the signal of Morse's transmitter. So he strung a mile and a half of wire between his vantage point and the target zone, and sat there pressing a button on his control whenever a shell headed out to explode one of the cars [*opposite*]—comfortably getting a series of pictures that, without ingenious thinking, could never have been made.   *Al Schneider* □

Long-distance control of a motorized camera is made possible by a relay switch—shown above with its protective plastic cap removed—which closes a contact when electric current activates its electromagnet (diagram, top). The use of the relay eliminates problems caused by voltage loss in a long-wire connection, permitting operation of a camera from as far as two miles away. When the photographer throws a switch, the battery beside him sends a current to the relay. Even though this signal is weakened by resistance in the long wire, the relay is so sensitive that it instantly closes a circuit that connects a battery next to the camera. Current from this battery, suffering no losses from any long-wire connection, is available at full strength to run the motorized camera.

Al Schneider has been the Equipment Section head of the LIFE Photo Lab since 1956. In addition to building novel devices, he presides over an inventory of photographic gear that includes hundreds of camera bodies, 150 Ascor 800-watt-second strobe units, and a variety of lenses ranging from a 7.5-ounce fisheye to a 60-pound, nine-foot 2,000mm.

RALPH MORSE: *Artillery Practice at Fort Sill*, 1970

Striking savagely from the sky, an artillery shell demolishes an old car during target practice at Fort Sill, Oklahoma. The rapid-shooting Hulcher camera that caught this paroxysm of exploding metal was only 75 yards from the target—but the photographer, Ralph Morse, was safely located a mile and a half away, operating the camera by the relay system shown on the opposite page.

The Experts' Ingenuity

Photographers have been performing visual sleight of hand ever since the days when the craft's earliest practitioners used to join several daguerreotypes together to simulate a single panoramic shot. This trickery was well intentioned—a healthy refusal to admit that certain kinds of pictures were not feasible. Today the impulse to do the impossible is stronger than ever, and the list of ingenious ploys seems to be endless: complicated multiple exposures add new layers to reality; cutout paper masks or even very long time exposures subtract an undesired part of a scene; a standard lens is extended and turned around for magnified pictures.

In skillful hands, even the most brazen manipulations may be virtually undetectable. For example, Joel Snyder recently wanted a picture of foggy weather. Since nature failed to supply fog that day, he manufactured it himself

(opposite). He used a commercially available filter that produces the illusion of fog by scattering light to a slight degree. Not content with its performance, he applied a thin coating of clear nail polish to the filter; then he dropped it into a glass of cold water before it had completely dried; this caused the polish to wrinkle, increasing the amount of light scatter that would occur. Finally he cut the filter in half and screwed it on the lens so that it would cover the upper part of the scene.

When Snyder took the picture, he framed the landscape in such a way that the bottom edge of the filter surface coincided with the bank at the side of the road, just below the horizon. The result: a hauntingly beautiful image whose strength is its duality—fuzzy, fog-swathed trees in the background and a perfectly sharp highway traffic arrow thrusting into the foreground.

For this picture of artificial fog hovering near Chicago's Inner Drive, a wide-angle 35mm lens was used; the exposure was 1/60 second at f/11 (no exposure compensation was made for the fog filter). The shot had to be made on an overcast day, for direct sunlight would have made the unfiltered foreground look markedly different from the filter-softened background.

JOEL SNYDER: *Inner Drive, Chicago, 1970*

A Ghostly View of a Live Concert

Necessity proved to be the mother of invention when Gerald Jacobson was covering a rock concert at Brandeis University in 1968. Assigned by a book publisher to photograph a group called The Blues Project, he had to select his vantage point beforehand, for he would be unable to move once the audience packed into the gymnasium. He decided not to stand at the back of the gym because he would be too far from the performers, and he did not want to shoot from directly in front of the temporary stage since that would have required him to shoot upward at a sharp angle, distorting the pictures. The only other alternative was to stand at the side of the stage.

However, when the concert got under way, it appeared that his choice was a mistake. From his position at the side he was shooting into the stage lights; furthermore, the angle offered mostly profiles and back-of-the-head views, neither of which appealed to him. Then he saw the solution. The lights—two enormous spots with mirrored reflectors—were mounted close together at the back of the gymnasium and were casting very sharp shadows of the performers on the backdrop. All the ingredients for a stunning picture were there: the lettered curtain indicating that this was a university concert, the gleaming, dominant shapes of the sound equipment, and the shadows—insubstantial and yet larger than life. By upsetting the familiar make-up of reality, he got a composition that demands a second and third look.

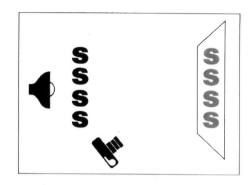

Only one musician (left) got his face into this picture; the others are represented by their shadows, cast by spotlights. The photograph was taken with a Leica equipped with a 28mm lens, and was exposed at 1/60 second at f/5.6. To emphasize the supernatural quality of the scene, high-contrast paper was used in printing.

GERALD JACOBSON: *Musicians' Shadows*, 1968

Switching Ordinary Equipment to Special Tasks

CARLO BAVAGNOLI: *Death of a Grasshopper*, 1967

The meat-eating driver ant, cousin of South America's dreaded army ant, devours everything in its path—chickens, snakes or grasshoppers like the one above being dispatched by a single soldier. The ants will eat human flesh too, but since they travel slowly in long, narrow columns, Bavagnoli was able to photograph them up close and then get away—although several of the tiny warriors hurled themselves onto his camera and had to be slapped away as he escaped.

When LIFE's Carlo Bavagnoli set out to do a story on the driver ants of Africa, he expected that he would have to invest in an expensive macro type of lens to get large, high-quality images of the small insects. He knew he could obtain magnified images with the normal 50mm lens on his Nikon by using extension rings to increase the lens-to-film distance, which controls image size. But some blurring of close-ups often results from such extension because it throws off the normal distance relationships between subject, lens and film.

To his delight, Bavagnoli found that he could reduce the blurring by using a special mounting ring and reversing his lens. (The same trick works with most 35mm cameras, provided the arrangement of glass components inside the lens is not symmetrical.) These improvisations provided sharp, larger-than-life-sized images that did justice to the ferocious ants.

CARLO BAVAGNOLI: *Soldier Ant's Mandibles*, 1967

The murderous mandibles of a soldier ant, the infantryman of the horde, are shown magnified approximately 20 times in an enlargment from a negative that itself was twice actual size. To create such large images, the lens was extended from its normal position by four metal rings and also mounted in a reversed position (left).

Turning the lens of the Nikon around helped avert pictures with blurred edges that sometimes result when a lens is placed very close to a subject. Any lens will work in a backwards position, but the distortion-clearing benefits will occur only with lenses whose glass elements are not symmetrically arranged.

1

2

3

4

5

6

The Experts' Ingenuity: continued

Totaling Up a Teacher's Workday

The same teacher appears six times in this multiple exposure, made with a view camera equipped with a wide-angle lens. Mounted in front of the camera on floodlight stands was a pane of glass to hold the paper masks that covered different parts of the scene for each exposure. Tests showed that the best results were obtained if the glass was positioned four inches in front of the lens—equal to the focal length of the lens. To prevent ghost images —caused by reflections between the two surfaces of the glass—two identically shaped masks were used, one on the front of the pane and the other the back. The mask sections farthest from the camera had to be 1/16 inch larger to allow for bending of light by the glass.

For a story on the nation's strained educational system, LIFE photographer Ralph Morse set his sights on a picture that flew in the face of good sense. He felt that the best way to illustrate the hectic job of a fifth-grade teacher was to show the teacher in several different places at once. This would have been fairly easy to do through multiple exposures if the teacher were in an empty room, but it seemed completely impractical in a roomful of restless students, who could not easily be kept from moving in the picture.

But after laborious experimentation, Morse devised a technique that brought off the illusion *(opposite).* He aimed his camera through a pane of glass that was covered by a mask made of several sections of black paper. Each section was attached to the glass by its own piece of double-stick tape—allowing the sections to be removed and replaced independently. Without changing the camera position, he made six exposures, removing a different section of the mask every time *(left),* so that each exposure caught only the portion of the schoolroom uncovered by that particular section. In between exposures, the teacher walked from one place to another; her course had been determined when the mask was made.

Most of the children did not have to remain motionless throughout, since they figured only in the first exposure *(top left)* taken with the largest section of the mask removed. But a few children appeared in later exposures, and they had to stay perfectly still. In these crucial spots, Morse placed students who were hand-picked for patience —since the complicated composition required three long minutes to make.

RALPH MORSE: *A Teacher's Tasks*, 1954

A Polite Way to Make People Vanish

Cathedrals, palaces and historic homes are favorite photographic subjects for the vacationer, but they pose one special difficulty: the photographer is not alone. Invariably other tourists are present and they will appear in the picture, adding a jarring, anachronistic note to the architectural splendors. Yet there is a way to erase the tourists, as if by magic. Evelyn Hofer used it for her photograph of the 1,000-year-old Baptistery in Florence *(opposite)*. Not a single person is in sight, even though the picture was taken at the peak of the tourist season, when hundreds of people were milling about in the building. They all have been eliminated by the simple tactic of making a very long time-exposure.

A long exposure was perfectly suited to Miss Hofer's purposes in any case. It allowed her to record the scene by the weak available light, without having to set up floodlights or resort to strobe or flash bulbs that might have given uneven lighting over such a large area. Also, an extra amount of exposure was required because she used a red filter to bring out the geometrical pattern of the two kinds of marble in the wall. Age had so darkened the white marble that it normally would have been hard to distinguish from the thin, decorative slabs of green marble; but a red filter —which blocks green light—turned the green slabs black and heightened the contrast in the wall. The combination of the filter and the dim light—plus her choice of a slow film—permitted her to keep the shutter open for 20 minutes. As a result, the moving people did not register on the film. However, she was not totally successful. One ghostlike streak can be seen in the lower left-hand corner of the picture. It was caused by a tourist who was apparently so transfixed by the architecture that he stayed in one spot several minutes. ☐

Passing crowds of tourists never show in a 20-minute exposure of the marble-lined Baptistery in Florence, taken with a 4 x 5 Linhof view camera mounted on a very steady tripod. Several factors made such a long exposure possible: the light coming through the opened entrance door was very dim; a red filter over the lens reduced the amount of light reaching the film by an amount equivalent to three or four f-stops; the aperture was set at a minimum opening of f/64; and the film was slow, ASA 64. ►

EVELYN HOFER: *Interior of Baptistery in Florence*, 1959

"Profit by My Mistakes"

Following is a first-person account of problems encountered by Mark Kauffman—and fellow photographers—during 34 years of picture taking:
I remember a conversation I had one day with Ed Thompson when he was managing editor of LIFE. I was showing him some pictures from a story I had shot, and I started telling him about some of the pictures I hadn't got because of camera failure. Ed interrupted me immediately. "Don't tell me about the pictures you *didn't* get," he said. "Just show me the good ones you *got*."

While the pictures you *didn't* get may be of no interest to a managing editor, they can be useful to you. In some cases they may be more useful than the pictures you *got*—if you can learn something from your mistakes.

Whether he admits it or not, every photographer makes mistakes. The good photographer is the one who figures out what happened and sees to it that it doesn't happen again. I have made plenty of mistakes in 34 years of taking pictures, and I've learned a lot from them. Let me tell you about some of my errors—and some that other LIFE photographers have made—in the hope that you can avoid making the same ones.

Backgrounds can be ruinous or embarrassing, or both. Very often the photographer gets so involved with his subject he doesn't see beyond it. A while back, I was assigned to do a story on the Broadway musical *Mame.* The show was a great success and my coverage of it came off well; LIFE planned to use several pages. Then the editors decided they wanted a two-page foldout cover of the show's star, Angela Lansbury. She agreed to come to the LIFE studio, but only for a quick session because she was exhausted from opening night and weeks of out-of-town rehearsals.

We felt the best cover try would be the scene in which Angela does a Groucho Marx trot across the stage holding a cigar, while dancers and acrobats whoop it up in the background. We arranged for hired limousines to pick up Angela and some of the cast and bring them to the LIFE studio. I promised to take no more than 30 minutes for the whole session.

I got to the studio early. With the help of three assistants I set up the strobe lights and made exposure and lighting tests and we were ready to go when they all arrived. I spent most of the time concentrating on Angela's expressions, trying to catch her at just the right moment as she did her trot across the studio stage. Behind her, four girls were doing high kicks, one after another in rapid succession to counterpoint the star's movements.

I sensed that something was disturbing in the background, but I was so involved with Angela's movements and with the time running out that I just shot away. After only 15 minutes we were forced to call it quits because everybody was exhausted from the fast-repeated takes. I shot about thirty 4 x 5 color sheets (the bigger format film would blow up better for a two-page cover). The film was processed and I sat down to edit the pictures.

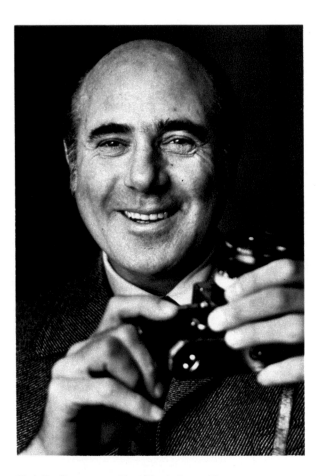

Mark Kauffman can smile at his photographic mistakes—he has earned the right. Ever since he made the cover of LIFE in 1939 with a sensitive picture of Eleanor Roosevelt, when he was still a high school student, Kauffman has been in the front rank of professionals. A LIFE photographer since 1945, he has gone to every corner of the globe to make photographs on such varied topics as wars, rebellions, politics, fashions, food, theater and sports.

The background was indeed disturbing. Evidently the four high-kicking girls take care when dressing for a stage performance to make sure they don't give the front-row customers more than their money's worth, but for some reason they had neglected to prepare as carefully for the picture taking. As I went through picture after picture, I found the chorus girls stealing the scene from the star. Out of the 30 pictures, there was only *one* that could be cropped in a way to keep the girls decent and yet focus on the star. It was used for the cover, but I learned from my mistake: keep your eye on what's happening in the background. It could be embarrassing.

My friend and fellow photographer John Dominis learned a somewhat similar lesson when he was making a picture of a tempting Spanish *paella* for the LIFE Great Dinners series. John thought he had a perfect set of pictures, until his color was processed and examined closely. There, sitting on top of the succulent rice and seafood dish was a common, everyday house fly. A new *paella* had to be whipped up and the pictures taken all over again, this time with several fly-frighteners standing by.

Lighting offers the photographer many golden opportunities for mistakes. Strobe lights, for example, have the nasty habit of firing on their own if several are incorrectly plugged together—when the connections are inadvertently reversed, a kind of short circuit is created and power flows before it is supposed to. This tendency in strobes has caused me more than a modicum of grief—particularly when I was photographing two short-tempered giants in their field: Pancho Gonzales, the master tennis player, and Kwame Nkrumah, the first prime minister of Ghana.

Gonzales was playing a professional tennis match at the old Madison Square Garden in New York. Knowing his volatile nature, I used my strobe lights sparingly so I would not break into his intense concentration. I had not plugged the strobes together correctly, however, and suddenly they all started firing at once. Gonzales, blinded by the lights, whirled on me, his mighty racket raised. His rage seemed to inflate his natural size and strength, inspiring vivid visions of my mortality. I quickly threw the strobes' emergency switch and doused the lights.

The episode with Nkrumah was even more terrifying. He had just become prime minister of the fledgling nation of Ghana when it attained its freedom in 1957. Now in power after years of political turbulence and struggle, Nkrumah was a deeply suspicious man. I was granted only a few minutes to take his picture. So as not to waste his time, I set up my strobes in his office at 7:30 a.m. to have them ready when he gave me the word to shoot. I was waiting in his anteroom when suddenly the door to his office flew open and the enraged prime minister rushed toward me shouting, "You are taking my picture secretly!" Speaking with the rapid eloquence that only terror can induce, I explained that strobes, like some women, were not known for their faithfulness. I somehow managed to calm the prime minister, got my pictures and kept myself from incarceration in a Ghanaian jail. The lesson is that although you may be more likely to photograph a tennis player than a prime minister, you should take care to avoid frightening and annoying your subject with incorrectly connected lights.

Of course, the best sort of mistake to learn from is the one that accidentally produces a better picture than you planned. LIFE photographer Henry Groskinsky told me about the time he was doing a story on the University of Toronto's astronomical observatory. He wanted to show the observatory's 74-inch telescope against a starry night sky, so he asked that the dome be opened. He was warned that it was about to snow, but he insisted the dome be opened anyway. His request was granted, the dome was opened and —sure enough—it began to snow. The snowflakes landing on Henry's banks of hot light bulbs made them explode like a row of firecrackers. He could save only one light. Instead of giving up, he shot his pictures with that one light. As it turned out, the pictures had a pleasant moonlit effect, much more natural than the picture his battery of lights might have produced. The color picture was good enough to be used as the cover for the *Planets* book in the LIFE Science Library.

Perhaps the last word on lighting should be given by the LIFE photographer and bon vivant, Alfred Eisenstaedt. After one of his many European photographic assignments, he was asked what he really did at night in Paris. Eisie deadpanned, "I expose longer."

Even the metallic click of a camera's shutter can spoil an intimate mood or a silent moment of concentration. A while back during a Masters golf tournament, the click of my camera consistently made me the recipient of dirty looks from officials and players. In those days, Ben Hogan and Sam Snead were among the top players. As I followed them around the tricky course in Augusta, Georgia, the noise of my camera was clearly distracting them. I figured that I had better do something before one of them wrapped a driver around my neck.

I was wiping my face with a hotel towel after shaving before the beginning of the second round, when a solution to the noise problem came to me: I would muffle the camera by wrapping it in the thick towel. I practiced in my hotel room until I could aim the heavily wrapped camera and take a picture. My sound-deadening towel worked. Snead won, Hogan was second and I didn't get a dirty look the rest of the tournament.

The most maddening mechanical mistake a photographer can make is to insert a new roll of film without fitting it correctly into the winding sprockets. You shoot, think you are advancing the film, shoot some more, and then

—only when you have "shot" an entire roll—you discover that your film has not advanced one frame the whole time. Instead of unforgettable photographs you have blanks. This happened to me once when I was shooting a story for LIFE. A camera assistant was working with me, and I made the unforgivable error of having him load the camera. A photographer should always load his own camera so that he has no one to blame but himself if anything goes wrong.

The assistant, who is now a very good professional photographer, didn't get the film started right on the take-up sprockets. The film never advanced. The counter clicked off the pictures even though the film remained stationary. All my shots went unrecorded and I had to do that part of the story all over again. If it had been a news event, I would have lost it completely. To avoid repeating this mistake, I adopted a trick that works on many makes of 35mm cameras. I leave the lever of the rewind knob sticking up. In this way, I can see the lever turning when the film is advancing.

Another mechanical problem I faced once was caused by an oversight on my part while covering a state dinner dance at the White House during the term of President Lyndon B. Johnson. The occasion was the visit of Princess Margaret of Great Britain and her husband, the photographer Antony Armstrong-Jones. LIFE had permission for exclusive coverage, and I went to Washington ahead of time with an assistant to take pictures of the staff and Mrs. Johnson preparing for the big night. When the evening for the dinner dance arrived, I was suddenly told I would not be allowed to take a tripod to the affair. The hosts were afraid that it would call attention to my presence as a photographer. I had not taken this into account when planning my coverage. The only special lighting in the East Room consisted of my two strobes bounced off the ceiling. And I knew I would have to use long exposures in order to get good color shots. Long exposures are easy with a tripod but are nearly impossible with a hand-held camera. The only way I could possibly handle the situation was to find something solid to put the camera on to keep it steady.

I settled on my tuxedo-clad assistant, placing him directly in front of me and using his shoulder as a tripod. He had to stand absolutely still and hold his breath whenever we needed a long exposure. The next day he showed me a black-and-blue welt on his right shoulder where I had repeatedly pressed the camera down to keep it steady. The story made the cover and 10 pages, and his shoulder should have gotten a by-line. President Johnson didn't help the situation, by the way; knowing I was photographing the event, he kept winking at me across the ballroom.

Moral: If you're planning to photograph an indoor party and want to be inconspicuous, plan to have something as steady as a tripod (a high-backed

chair, for example) but less obvious ready at hand. And watch out for wink-
ers; they can spoil your pictures too.

Too much light, remember, can be even worse than not enough light. Once
I was doing a baseball story in Cuba (long ago when you could do baseball
stories in Cuba), and made the mistake of leaving one of my cameras on a
bench bordering the playing field. The lens was pointed up, right at the sun.
The lens, acting just like a Boy Scout's magnifying glass, focused a bright,
hot image of the sun onto the camera focal plane, where the cloth shutter
covers the film. It burned a nice little hole right through the shutter so that
light could reach the film underneath. All of the pictures taken with this camera had a bright white spot in the middle. I wasn't aware of it, of course, but
when the film was shipped unprocessed to New York, I got a cable right away
from Bill Sumits, then head of the LIFE darkroom. "YOU'VE GOT A HOLE IN
SHUTTER OF ONE OF YOUR CAMERAS LEAVING SPOT ON FILM. MUST
HAVE BEEN LEFT FACING SUN." When I got back to New York, I asked
Sumits how he detected it so quickly. He said, "Made the same mistake
years ago in Kansas."

Ever since then I've been careful to leave my cameras and film in the
shade. Not only can the sun burn through a shutter, but the sun's heat can
get at your film and change its color—sometimes it turns a sickly red, so bad
that you can't even pretend you "wanted that red for effect." I guess the
worst time I had with the sun was on an assignment in the Jordanian desert. I
was covering director David Lean while he was filming the movie *Lawrence
of Arabia.* I remember the star, Peter O'Toole, remarking, "There goes Kauffman playing the shade game again," while I scurried around trying to keep
my cameras out of that blazing sun.

The *Lawrence of Arabia* cameramen let me keep my main supply of film in
the only available air-conditioned van, which had been brought along to
keep their movie film cool. Every day I took just what I thought I'd need for
that day, and then the "shade game" would begin. I spent more time during
the day finding some little shadow in which to park my equipment than I did
taking pictures. Bringing my own umbrella with me would have saved me a
lot of unnecessary trouble and worry. To top it off, I managed to forget another lesson, one I thought I had learned earlier in northern Minnesota in the
dead of winter—keep your film warm as well as cool. As is the case in all des-
erts, the temperature drops drastically when the sun goes down; in Jordan
it plunged from 120° at noon to 45° or lower at dusk. The cold, combined
with the drop in humidity, produced lines of static electricity right across the
film. So the lesson is: don't let your film get overheated or overcold, even if it
means walking along a beach with an umbrella, or carrying rolls of film under
your shirt in ski country.

Viki, Kauffman's most difficult living subject, was bathed daily by her psychologist "mother," Mrs. Keith J. Hayes (upper left), in an experiment designed to test the capacity for learning in a chimpanzee raised like a human child. After the morning tub, Viki would cavort around the bathroom before dressing.

One of the commonest mistakes many a photographer makes in shooting where there are crowds of people is to assume that he has an advantageous location, only to discover how wrong he is. In a stadium covering a boxing match, I was under the impression that I had the perfect spot for picture taking. I did, as long as the crowd remained seated. But during the dramatic high point of the fight the crowd naturally rose like a wave in front of me and I was left with stunning pictures of the backs of people's heads. I have learned that a handy piece of equipment in these situations is a small portable stepladder. Alfred Eisenstaedt, who stands all of five feet tall, has his own way of seeing over crowds. Unable to see clearly the inauguration of President Dwight D. Eisenhower in 1953, Eisie asked the girl reporter accompanying him to bend down. He then climbed up on her shoulders, and, as she straightened up, he snapped his pictures from his human perch. I'm six feet and weigh 185 pounds—I use a ladder.

Photographers can also commit errors in not giving their subjects a complete fill-in on what they want to do. I once narrowly escaped an onslaught by the beautiful but fiery actress Melina Mercouri just because I neglected to tell her all the details of my photographic mission. My assignment concerned a movie that starred several lovely actresses—including Miss Mercouri and Romy Schneider. I had shot Miss Mercouri first, and on the following day I started taking pictures of Miss Schneider. She proved a difficult subject, reluctant to pose. But after some experience photographing Hollywood actresses, I had had the foresight to bring along a well-chilled bottle of champagne. After a few sips, Romy became more animated and I took some lively pictures. Then trouble arose: Melina happened along and saw me with another actress—and the champagne. Her temper flaring, she all but flew at my eyes. It turned out that she assumed I hadn't liked the pictures I had made of her. I hurriedly explained that I was photographing *all* the actresses, not just her. If I had told her this at the outset, there wouldn't have been such an embarrassing scene.

But Melina was no problem at all compared to Viki. Viki was a chimpanzee; a Florida psychologist, Keith J. Hayes, and his wife had brought the chimp up just as parents would their own child, in a carefully controlled experiment to see how human a chimp can get. I was warned ahead of time that I must be very polite and understanding with the little beast, so as not to upset the experiment. It sounded like fun. Little did I realize that the chimp would have most of the fun.

At the Hayes's home, Viki met me at the door, took my hand and led me into the living room. As I chatted with the Hayeses, Viki sat on my lap. Slowly she pushed her long, bony finger up my nose. As I started to squirm away, Hayes cautioned me to let Viki do whatever she wanted. "We try to treat Viki exactly like a child," he explained. Viki seemed to enjoy having her finger up my nose because she kept it there until I felt blood beginning to trickle down my nostril. I also began to sweat, whereupon Viki lost interest in the inside of my nose and turned her attention to my beaded, balding brow. She crawled up on my chest and started to lick my forehead. When she tired of that, she dropped to the floor, pulled off my shoes and clumped around the room in them. It was like that for four days. I ate with Viki and talked with her—in somewhat limited conversations since her vocabulary was confined to such words as "cup" and "mama." I even took her to a drive-in movie. She grew quite fond of me, but for my part I was happy to end the one-sided romance as soon as I had my pictures. My mistake was in assuming that such a subject would be easy to photograph. I've learned that *any* subject can turn out to be difficult to cover, and a photographer should be prepared for every imaginable hazard and inconvenience, even including the affectionate attentions of a chimpanzee.

Without doubt, the most unnecessary mistake photographers consistently make is neglecting to see a picture that is begging to be taken. If I have ever been guilty of that error I will not want to acknowledge it, even in jest. But I'll never forget one scene that another photographer almost ruined for me. We were in the locker room of the old Brooklyn Dodgers just after they had lost the World Series to the New York Yankees in 1952. Sitting alone on a trunk, tears streaming down his face, was the Dodgers' fine infielder, Jackie Robinson. His face spoke volumes on what it means to a dedicated ballplayer to lose. I had time to catch only a few pictures of him before a newspaper photographer strode up to him, shattering the mood, and asked Jackie if he would come across the room to pose with manager Chuck Dressen. Evidently the newspaper photographer wanted both men to stand gaping at each other and looking sad. He was oblivious of the great picture he had missed —and had come close to ruining for me.

And then there is the "mistake" that really isn't one at all. I was once with my family at a public swimming pool in Washington, D.C., taking shots of my daughters to send to grandparents on both sides of the Atlantic (my wife is Finnish). As I was taking those family snapshots, I noticed a boy, about 12 years old, jumping off the diving board in his own special way. He would run off the board, leap straight into the air, and squirt water from his mouth as he came down. I took him at the height of his act. The print looked so charmingly ridiculous I sent it to the editor at LIFE in charge of the Miscellany page, the spot for unusual photos that was used to end the magazine. The picture ran, with the headline, "A Squirt in the Sun." I've been told that it is one of the all-time favorites of Miscellany page photographs. The picture was a random shot; but it was no mistake.

Mark Kauffman ☐

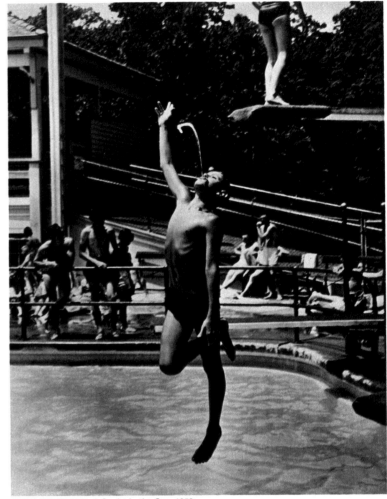

MARK KAUFFMAN: *A Squirt in the Sun*, 1953

The antics of a boy jumping off a diving board in a Washington, D.C., public swimming pool caught Kauffman's eye when he was there taking pictures of his daughters at play. Usually Kauffman considers working at photography during off hours an error to be avoided at all costs, but he snapped the boy and the result proved to be no "mistake." It appeared in LIFE in 1953 under the title "A Squirt in the Sun" and has remained to this day one of the photographer's most popular pictures.

Mechanical Failure 4

Techniques of Troubleshooting 102

How Sharp Is a Lens? 104

Simple Tests for Lenses 106

How Precise Is a Shutter? 108

Checking Synchronization of Strobe and Shutter 110

The Professionals' Tests 112

How the Prints Show What Went Wrong 114

Vignetting—The Lost Corners 116

Dirty Lens, Smudged Picture 117

Why a Shutter Misses Part of a Picture 118

Pictures Lost by Light 120

Disasters in Processing 122

Tracing Lines of Static 124

KODAK

→31A →32

GERALD JACOBSON: *Double Exposure Portrait*, 1969

Techniques of Troubleshooting

In February 1968, as debate raged throughout the nation over American bombing raids in Southeast Asia, LIFE photographer Co Rentmeester arrived at a United States air base in Guam with a satchelful of sophisticated camera equipment. His plan was to fly aboard a B-52 bomber on a mission over North and South Vietnam, and to take pictures as the jet dropped its bomb load on Communist supply lines and ammo depots. To catch the bombs at the very moment that they spewed from the belly of the aircraft, he fitted remote controls to a motorized Nikon and installed it in a wing. Sixteen hours of painstaking work were needed to attach the camera and to lead its triggering cable through the wing to the cabin where he would sit. It hardly seemed worth it in the end. He flew three high-altitude missions, but each time, despite winterizing, his camera froze. Only by mounting a second motorized Nikon in the warmer bomb bay and by shooting when the bay doors opened and the bombs were released, did Rentmeester manage to come back with the kind of picture he was after.

Camera malfunction is probably the photographer's blackest nightmare. Whether the trouble lies with the expensive, specialized equipment of a professional like Rentmeester or with an amateur's standard gear, the effects in lost time and wasted pictures can be heartbreaking. Many things can go wrong. In the camera, the metal springs that close shutters can lose their tension. A sharp jolt can wreck a focusing system by knocking lens elements out of alignment. Parts can deteriorate from long use. The mechanism that simultaneously advances the film and cocks the shutter can wear out, resulting in multiple double exposures. The retractable mirror in a single-lens reflex, situated directly behind the lens to allow the photographer to focus, can fail to pull back when the shutter is tripped, so that the image never reaches the film and no exposure takes place. Continuous vibrations from an automobile or airplane can shake parts loose in a camera. LIFE science photographer Fritz Goro, shooting pictures of an archeological dig in Guatemala in 1963, produced several rolls of light-struck negatives. A tiny fitting in the base of his Rolleiflex had vibrated loose during the helicopter flight to the dig, so that sunlight streamed into his camera like the beam from a miniature flashlight. If Goro had not backed up his Rollei pictures by taking additional shots with another camera, his assignment would have been a total failure.

Many such disasters become apparent only after the pictures have been processed, and close study of prints is often the best way to detect malfunctions. But the professional tries to prevent trouble by periodically testing his equipment. Before setting out on an assignment he often aims his camera out a window and focuses on a distant building to make sure that the image is sharp when the focusing scale indicates infinity. By opening the back of the camera, looking through the lens and clicking the shutter, he can see whether the shutter opens and closes smoothly. He makes sure that the batteries in their flash units and light meters operate effectively. After loading a 35mm camera, he can tell whether the film will run through smoothly by clicking off a few frames, and seeing if the rewind knob turns as he cocks the film-advance lever. For a more exhaustive check-out, working photographers send their cameras to a repair shop. Some publications maintain their own. *The National Geographic* magazine, for example, considers testing so important that it asks photographers to turn in their equipment for a thorough checkup after each assignment. And some manufacturers send teams of experts from the factory to major scheduled news events, such as moon shots and political conventions, to offer free testing and repair service to the professionals on assignment there.

Repairmen rely on a battery of complex optical and electronic equipment *(pages 112-113)* to ensure the accuracy of their tests. Oscilloscopes trace a graph on a screen to indicate exactly how long a shutter stays open at each setting. Battery testers determine the strength of flash batteries, and a lamp with an opal-glass screen and a dial for regulating light intensity allows technicians to make certain that light meters register correctly for all degrees of brightness. But such special equipment is not really necessary for most tests. Much information can be discovered at home by an amateur with no more equipment than a few charts, a tape measure, several rolls of film, phosphorescent tape and a magnifying glass.

Do-it-yourself tests like those that follow, applied either to the camera itself or to pictures made with the camera, can reveal most common defects. They are invaluable for detecting hidden faults in newly purchased cameras and lenses, particularly if the equipment is bought secondhand. And they also provide a convenient way of checking out a favorite old camera, indicating if it should go to the repair shop before a once-in-a-lifetime photographic opportunity is lost.

How Sharp Is a Lens?

The heart of a camera is its lens. Finely constructed shutters, precise focusing systems, lightproof, sturdy housings —all will be of little help to the photographer in search of fine pictures if his camera lacks a good lens, or if his lens has somehow got out of adjustment. Camera manufacturers are so particular about the quality of their lenses that they often take as much trouble testing them as they do making them. Before a new lens design goes into production, manufacturers sometimes spend weeks testing a prototype, probing it with light rays and laser beams, feeding hundreds of statistics into computers for evaluation. Later, as finished lenses leave production lines, they are tested again to make sure they conform to the same high standard as the prototype.

Even so, no lens is ever perfect. The most carefully constructed lenses will have certain built-in aberrations because of the peculiar ways in which light rays travel through curved pieces of glass. Images will be sharper at certain apertures than at others, and they will usually be sharper at the center than at the edges. Some lenses will produce clearer images with blue light rays than with yellow ones, and some are particularly likely to pick up unwanted flashes of reflected light, or flare. Though none of these faults can be eliminated entirely, lens-makers rely on testing to make sure they are kept to a practical minimum.

One basic test evaluates lens resolution—the ability of the lens to render detail; it can be carried out by the amateur, as described on pages 106-107. The test determines how many lines per millimeter the lens can distinguish at a prescribed distance from a target. There are a number of different versions. One pattern, for instance, was developed for the U.S. Air Force to test lenses used in aerial reconnaissance, where good detail is essential. But all versions of the resolution test are carried out in basically the same way, by photographing a wall chart covered with a number of carefully designed test patterns. Each test pattern (one example is shown opposite) consists of groups of lines of different sizes separated by varying widths of blank space. The developed negative is examined through a magnifying glass. The groups of larger lines will appear sharp, but some of the smaller groups will blur into each other. The smallest group that the lens is able to separate into clearly defined lines and blank spaces will be a measure of its resolving power.

Many variables besides the quality of the lens may affect the results of the resolution test. The film used and the process by which it is developed both influence the sharpness of the negatives. More significant, perhaps, is the fact that the test may uncover defects in the camera body or the focusing system. An uneven lens mount, a pressure plate at the back of the camera that does not hold the film firmly in the focal plane, or an inaccurate range finder all create a telltale blurring in the lines of the test patterns.

A test pattern, designed during the Korean War to check the resolving power of Air Force camera lenses, is shown enlarged 2½ times. It consists of 24 groups of lines of diminishing size, with each group containing three vertical lines and three horizontal ones. A number of such patterns arranged on a wall form the target for the resolution test. The numerals next to each line group refer to a table that lists the resolution in lines per millimeter.

Simple Tests for Lenses

Using a resolution chart to test the sharpness of a lens requires the utmost accuracy and care. The camera must be properly placed, lighting must be precise, and the film must be developed in a specified manner. But an amateur, following the right procedures, not only can determine a lens's resolving power, but can check it for various types of distortion and aberration as well.

The first step is positioning the camera and chart. (Opposite, at left, is a negative of one standard chart, consisting of 16 test patterns arranged in a cross.) The camera must be placed securely on a tripod at a distance from the chart of 26 times the focal length of the lens. Thus, a two-inch (50mm) lens should be 52 inches away from the chart; a six-inch (150mm) lens should be 156 inches away.

The camera should be loaded with a high-resolution film, such as Panatomic-X, and a series of exposures made, one at each f-stop, while the shutter speed is adjusted so that the exposures remain constant. After exposure, the film should be carefully developed in a fine-grain developer.

The results of the test must be read directly from the negative through a magnifying glass. Using an enlarger to make a print would add another variable—the enlarger's lens—and could give misleading results for the camera lens. With the Photo-Lab-Index chart shown here, resolution in lines per millimeter is indicated by numbers next to each group of lines in the test patterns. To obtain the lens's resolving power, read the smallest group of lines in each test pattern that the lens is able to differentiate clearly.

Test results can tell more about a lens than just its overall sharpness. Almost all lenses have an unavoidable defect called spherical aberration. This means that they tend to form sharper images with the light rays that come through the center than with the rays that enter through the edges. Therefore, the negatives taken at the smaller apertures, where the edges are blocked off by the diaphragm, will probably show greater resolution than negatives taken at wide-open apertures. A careful examination of the negatives reveals which apertures will produce the least spherical aberration—and thus the sharpest pictures—in a given lens.

Other defects may show up on the negatives. The test patterns at the corners of the chart may be fuzzier than the ones near the center, indicating that the sharpest image the lens forms is curved slightly. Astigmatism—inability of a lens to reproduce horizontal and vertical lines equally well at the same time—shows up because the lines in each test pattern run at right angles to one another. Finally, a glance at the three long lines that frame the edges of the chart may show that the lens distorts images. If the lines bow inward the lens suffers from what is known as pincushion distortion; an outward bowing means barrel distortion *(opposite, top)*.

Standardized test charts, which give an accurate, numerical reading of a lens's resolving power, are available through most camera supply shops. But even without a chart an amateur can estimate the quality of his lens by substituting another flat surface with right-angle lines, such as a brick wall *(opposite)*. While the results are not as exact, they provide clues to many of the same defects that test charts show.

Accurate positioning of camera and lights is essential for getting good results from a test chart. The camera's lens must be centered exactly opposite the center of the chart, as shown above. If the camera is set at the slightest angle to left or right, or tilted up or down the smallest bit, the test will be misleading. Lights should be placed to provide even, glare-free illumination. In the arrangement shown here, two 15-watt frosted bulbs set in satin-finish reflectors are placed on either side of the camera at an angle of approximately 45°.

The test results for one lens, obtained from both a Photo-Lab-Index chart (left) and a brick wall, show barrel distortion. The parallel lines on the top and bottom edges of the chart, and the upper and lower rows of bricks, are bowed.

Another test from a different lens shows no sign of distortion. This particular lens also seems to have a greater resolving power than the lens tested at the top, since details in both the chart and the brick wall appear to be much sharper.

How Precise Is a Shutter?

While shutters on modern cameras are quite durable, they sometimes wear out. There are two common types of shutter. In one, the leaf type, thin metal blades slide from the center of the shutter and move toward its perimeter to open and slide back to close. In the focal-plane type, by contrast, a pair of curtains with an adjustable opening between them sweeps across the film, from one side of the camera to the other. Both shutter types are operated by springs. With age, the springs lose their springiness, making the shutter move more slowly than it should. Thus at a setting of 1/500 second the shutter may stay open twice that time, producing overexposed pictures.

Other faults throw shutters off their timing. A complicated arrangement of gears and levers regulates the speed. If one gear works loose or wears out, the shutter may not function properly at a particular setting. The mechanism may become clogged with dirt, causing the shutter to move unevenly. In each instance exposures become erratic.

One way to test shutter mechanisms is to take a series of pictures of the same subject under the same light conditions, one at each shutter speed, while changing the f-stop so that the total amount of light reaching the film remains constant. If one frame is odd —significantly lighter or darker than the others *(opposite)*—either the shutter does not work at that speed, or the diaphragm is out of adjustment at that f-stop. The diaphragm can be ruled out if, in a second test series shot with a different set of graduated shutter/f-stop combinations, another odd frame turns up at the same shutter speed that produced the first odd frame.

To check the shutter speeds on a camera, an evenly lighted street scene like the one on these pages makes a good test subject. A series of pictures was shot at different combinations of shutter speeds and diaphragm openings, beginning with 1/30 second at f/16 (top, opposite), then 1/60 second at f/11 (center, opposite), and so on up to 1/1000 second at f/2.8 (bottom, this page). Since f-stop changes compensated for shutter-speed changes in each case, density of the resulting pictures should have been almost identical. But one, shot at 1/500 second at f/4 (center, this page), was obviously overexposed. To make certain that it was the shutter and not the diaphragm that malfunctioned at that setting, another set of exposures was made, beginning with f/22 at 1/30 second. The camera again overexposed at 1/500 (with an f-stop of f/5.6), clear proof that the shutter was the mechanism that needed repair.

Checking Synchronization of Strobe and Shutter

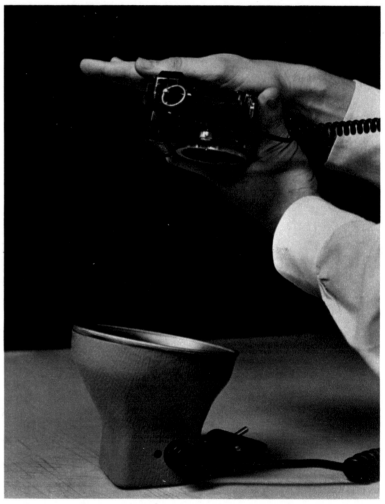

To test a focal-plane shutter for strobe synchronization, a 1½-by-2-inch piece of phosphorescent tape, which glows after being exposed to light, is held (above), phosphorescent side toward the lens, in the place where film would normally be. Next, with the flash unit's synchronization cord connected to the camera and the shutter set at 1/60 second —the usual speed for strobe—the camera is aimed at the unit and the shutter snapped (right). The tape is then inspected (opposite) to see if the entire frame was uniformly exposed.

Another camera part that must operate with extreme precision is the mechanism that synchronizes the shutter with a strobe attachment. If the timing of either shutter or flash is off by as little as a few thousandths of a second, the result will be a loss of part of the negative if the camera uses a focal-plane shutter, or an underexposed negative if the camera has a leaf shutter.

With either type of shutter, the strobe flash is designed to go off at almost —but not quite—the same instant that the shutter is tripped. A tiny moment of hesitation is purposely built into the synchronization device. This gives the shutter time to open up completely before the light reaches the film. The leaves of a leaf shutter, radiating out from its center, must be fully dilated; otherwise insufficient light will reach the film, causing the underexposure. To test such a shutter simply set the diaphragm wide, open the camera back, aim at the flash unit and watch the shutter open as the flash fires. If synchronization is correct, a perfectly round bright spot will be seen.

The problem is different in a camera equipped with a focal-plane shutter. Both of its curtains start out at one side of the window. When the shutter is tripped at the flash-sync setting, the first curtain travels across the window, opening it completely; at this point it closes the circuit that fires the flash.

Then the second curtain follows to close the window. But if the light unit fires too late—after the second curtain has started to move, covering one end of the frame—only a part of the film will be fully exposed and the rest of the negative will be blank.

A slow shutter speed (usually 1/60 second) is needed to make the curtain open fully and expose every part of the frame at once, admitting light from the strobe to all sections of the film. For this reason, only at these slow speeds can a focal-plane shutter be synchronized with strobe.

A simple way to test synchronization of a focal-plane shutter is to take a "picture" of the flash itself (left). Instead of film, photographers use a piece of phosphorescent tape, available through hardware stores at nominal cost. With the back of the camera open, the tape is held in the spot where the film would normally be (opposite, far left), and the shutter is set at the speed recommended for strobe. The photographer shoots directly into the camera's flash unit (left). If the flash is synchronized with the shutter, it will leave an afterglow on the tape that fills the frame; otherwise the glow may be only a sliver (right). The fault could be nothing more than a mistake in setting the shutter to the speed for strobe synchronization; but if that can be ruled out, the mechanism needs repair.

Light patterns on phosphorescent tape reveal whether strobe and focal-plane shutter were synchronized or, if not, how drastically they were out of step. In the example at the top, where the light pattern covers the entire picture frame, the flash was properly timed to go off when the shutter was completely open. But in the other examples the flash fired late, when the shutter was no longer fully open.

The Professionals' Tests

Professional camera technicians use many of the same tests that an amateur does, using charts and measuring tape. But for a more elaborate check-out, they maintain an arsenal of equipment.

There are instruments for measuring the amperage in electronic flash batteries and the current that powers motorized cameras. Microscopes can reveal whether scratches in negatives were the result of irregularities in the camera. Another optical device, called an auto-collimator *(third picture at right)*, lets a repairman look inside a closed camera directly through its lens and watch an image being formed in the film plane; it gives an instant reading on the camera's focusing ability and a quick way to check lenses for their propensity to flare *(pages 56-57)* and for various types of optical distortion. Still other instruments are used to measure shutter speeds and to reveal shutter bounce *(pages 118-119)*, and one, a device for testing flash synchronization *(right)*, uses virtually the same principle as the phosphorescent tape test *(pages 110-111)* to test shutter timing for both strobe units and flash bulbs. □

The professional way to gauge flash synchronization—for both strobe units and flash bulbs—is to connect the camera to a $200 Synchro-Tester. For a test of the strobe setting, the camera, with back removed, is aimed at the machine's opal-glass screen and the shutter clicked. The tester's built-in light should flash, brightening its screen, at the same instant that the shutter opens fully (above, left); if the shutter is only partly open (above, right), then the sync mechanism is malfunctioning. When testing the synchronization of flash bulbs, which take a few thousandths of a second to reach peak intensity, a dial is set to delay the tester's light burst; otherwise the test is the same as that used for strobe synchronization.

An $800 piece of gadgetry called a motion analyzer gives an exact picture of a camera's shutter action. The camera, its lens and back removed, is placed on a special stand. When the shutter is tripped, light from the overhead lamp floods through the shutter opening to a photoelectric cell. The cell sends current to an oscilloscope (upper left on the instrument panel), which translates it into a graphic representation of the speed and smoothness with which the shutter opens and closes.

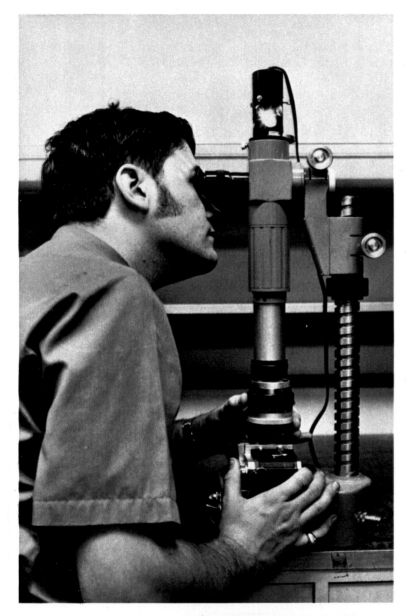

To test a Nikon's focusing system, LIFE camera technician Mike Miller places the camera, lens upward, under the cylinder of an auto-collimator. A light beams from the cylinder's top past a target and through the camera's lens, throwing the target's image onto the camera's film plane. At the same time, an eyepiece lets Miller peer directly into the camera through its lens and judge the sharpness of the image.

How the Prints Show What Went Wrong

No matter how thoroughly a photographer checks his equipment in advance, the acid test of its performance is the prints the negatives produce. A quick glance at a set of contact sheets is sometimes all that is necessary to reveal many of these mechanical failures. When prints are unevenly shaded, double exposed or marred with light spots or dark patches, a bit of armchair detective work can often determine exactly what went wrong.

Double exposures, like those opposite, are quickly spotted in contact sheets. Such mishaps are simply not supposed to happen with most modern roll-film cameras. Virtually all are provided with a single lever that both cocks the shutter and advances the film to bring a fresh frame into taking position. Thus the shutter cannot operate to take a picture unless the film has also been moved, theoretically protecting photographers from an error that occurred rather frequently in the past —forgetting to wind the film between shots. But if the mechanism malfunctions, so that the film does not advance a full frame when the shutter is cocked, double or overlapping exposures are inevitable, no matter how careful the photographer is.

Even if the film-advance device operates normally, too much tension on the film can also prevent it from moving. This excessive tension results occasionally if the film has been improperly packaged and does not roll smoothly out of the magazine or off the spool; too much tension may also be produced by the camera's own rewind device, which can jam and cause a drag that holds back the moving film. The same kind of drag sometimes occurs in damp weather, when moisture condenses on the pressure plate, which is designed to keep the film flat as it passes through the back of the camera; the moisture makes the film stick to the plate.

The evidence of the contact sheet can solve many other mysteries of what went wrong. Multiple exposures on the first few negatives and blanks everywhere else on the roll suggest the film stopped moving entirely, perhaps because its forward end slipped out of the take-up spool; a series of partially overlapping exposures, on the other hand, could signify slippage in the mechanism or drag on the film. If the prints show blank white areas, indicating the film was struck unintentionally by light, the extent and location of the light-struck sections may reveal how the leak occurred—around the edges of a bent back, through a hole in a focal-plane shutter *(page 96),* past the incomplete protection of a faulty cassette.

The clues of the contact sheets can lead the photographic detective to deduce that equipment is not broken but misused. Consistent over- or underexposure in the prints may indicate an incorrect setting for film speed; a few underexposed shots in sequence could mean a filter forgotten on the lens (altered unnatural tonal values in those scenes would clinch that solution); blank corners give away the use of an undersized sunshade or misfit lens. Such failures are mechanical malfunctions, too—a breakdown in the essential link between the human photographer and his responsive machine.

→14 →14A →15

The overlapping exposures that showed up in this contact sheet seem to warn of trouble in the film-advance system of the camera. It was a camera in which a small button disengages the forward-moving take-up spool so that exposed film can be wound back into its cassette. But the photographer inadvertently misused it: he happened to press the rewind button as he cocked the shutter, thus allowing the film-advance mechanism to slip a bit so it only advanced the film about two thirds of a frame.

Vignetting—The Lost Corners

Interchangeable lenses, generally considered one of the most convenient features of many cameras, share a built-in hazard: in practice, not all of them are completely interchangeable. A lens may fit into the mount of a camera, yet chop off part of the picture—a phenomenon called vignetting *(right)*, in which the corners of a picture are underexposed or blank because the lens forms an image that is too small to cover the entire negative. The problem may escape notice when the lens is being used—the corners of some cameras' viewing screens often appear dark anyway—but it quickly becomes apparent on the contact sheet.

Vignetting also occurs when a lens is used with a filter or lens shade that is too small for it. The 28mm wide-angle lens on a 35mm camera, for example, "sees" everything in front of the camera included within an angle of about 75°. It needs a lens shade that flares outward sufficiently to avoid blocking any of this region. If the lens were fitted with a shade designed for a very long lens, which takes in a much smaller angle of view, part of the image that the lens transmits would be blocked off.

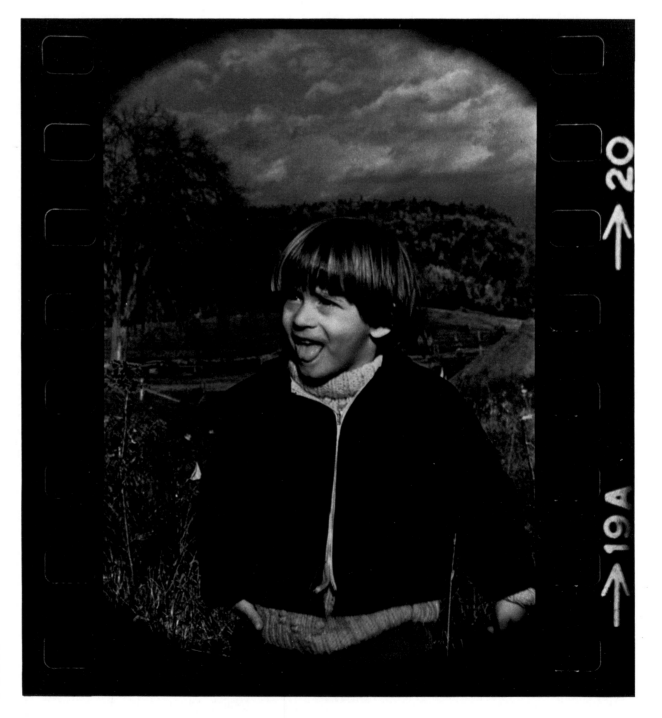

A picture without corners resulted when the photographer inadvertently fitted a long, narrow shade designed for a 105mm lens to his normal 55mm lens. The shade blocked out part of the image as effectively as blinders on a horse.

KODAK TRI X PAN FILM

A →13 →13A →14 →14

The print at the left clearly shows a seal basking in the sun at Central Park Zoo in New York: a fingerprint on the filter used during the taking of the next shot turned it and the seal into a meaningless blur. Although picture-ruining smears are easy to acquire and difficult to see, lenses and filters should be wiped off as seldom as possible, and then cautiously (they get scratched). Blow loose dust off before wiping. One of the best cleaning materials is nothing but a very old, freshly laundered handkerchief—the many washings in its past will have removed all lint that might otherwise stick to a lens.

Soot, grease marks, drops of moisture, lint from a handkerchief—all diffuse the light that passes through a lens or a filter, softening the focus of the image as it appears on a contact sheet. Sometimes photographers cultivate this kind of softness for effect, by covering their lenses with a translucent cloth, a filter smeared with grease or a diffusion disk —a sheet of glass incised with tiny grooves. But most pictures require the clear, precise detail that results only from clean lenses and filters.

Attempts to clean the lens may cause more trouble than the dirt, however. Rubbing the lens with a rough cloth produces a maze of fine scratches that softens images as effectively as the lines of a diffusion disk.

Even when its front and back surfaces are clean, a lens may lose sharpness because of internal dirt. In smoggy or humid climates, soot filters into the interior through the focus- and aperture-adjustment rings. If internal dirt is suspected—the exterior surface is clean and the lens and focusing system in order *(pages 104-107)*—a simple test should be made. Shine the beam of a pencil flashlight through the lens while examining it from the other side. If a layer of grayish scum can be seen on the interior surfaces, take the lens to a repair shop for cleaning.

Why a Shutter Misses Part of a Picture

Nothing is more disappointing than to take only half a picture. Yet this is exactly what may happen when the focal-plane shutter of a camera does not act the way the photographer expects. In both these sets of contact sheets, part of the image is lopped off because of shutter problems.

As the curtains that constitute the elements of a focal-plane shutter sweep from one side of the camera to the other, permitting light to enter through the space between them, they are rolled up on a rotating shaft, which must occasionally be readjusted by a repairman. Sometimes the first curtain will bounce back slightly when it reaches the shaft, blocking light—a phenomenon known as first-curtain shutter bounce. This is what has happened in the top sequence, cutting off a small part of each picture. At other times, a larger part of the picture may be lost because tension on the rotating shaft is too weak; the first curtain moves so slowly that the second curtain catches up with it before it has reached the far edge of the window. The opening closes prematurely, blocking the light from the edge of the picture—as a contact-sheet inspection would reveal.

The contact strip at the bottom, taken with a strobe flash, suggests that flash and shutter were out of synchronization or that the shutter speed was improperly set. Either fault *(test described on pages 110-111)* will prevent the shutter curtains from opening fully to expose the entire frame during the brief flash—and either one will cause a loss of part of the picture.

A focal-plane shutter that moved erratically blocked exposure along one edge of these portraits, taken at 1/125 second. Careful cropping could save the pictures.

Partial exposures always result when focal-plane shutters are improperly synchronized with electronic flash. These pictures were taken at too fast a shutter speed.

Pictures Lost by Light

Light makes a photograph but it can destroy one, too. If it leaks into the film compartment, it may wash away the images on an entire roll, or ruin a considerable number of pictures on the roll. The top strip at right shows a candlelit scene at a New York night club, shot with a Nikon F whose back had warped slightly. Light filtered through to bleach a scallop along the edge of the film. The fogged strip on the contact sheet reveals not only the existence of this light leakage but, by its location, suggests the source—the top of the camera back, since photographed images are always inverted within the camera.

The series at the bottom, taken to illustrate a book on rock musicians, shows an even more disastrous effect of light striking exposed film. The photographer, shooting away during the rock session, became worried that film was not winding onto the take-up spool when he cocked the film-advance lever —a situation that would have caused double exposures *(pages 114-115)*. To be certain that he had a functioning camera for the rest of the session, he risked opening the back of the camera —and ruined a number of his pictures, as the contact sheet made abundantly and unhappily clear.

Even the dim illumination of a candlelit
nightclub was sufficient to burn out the edges
of a film sequence that had been shot after
the back of the camera sprang a light leak.

Alternating sections of burned-out film are the
result of opening the back of a loaded
camera. They occurred because the photographer
checked to see if the film was jammed.

Disasters in Processing

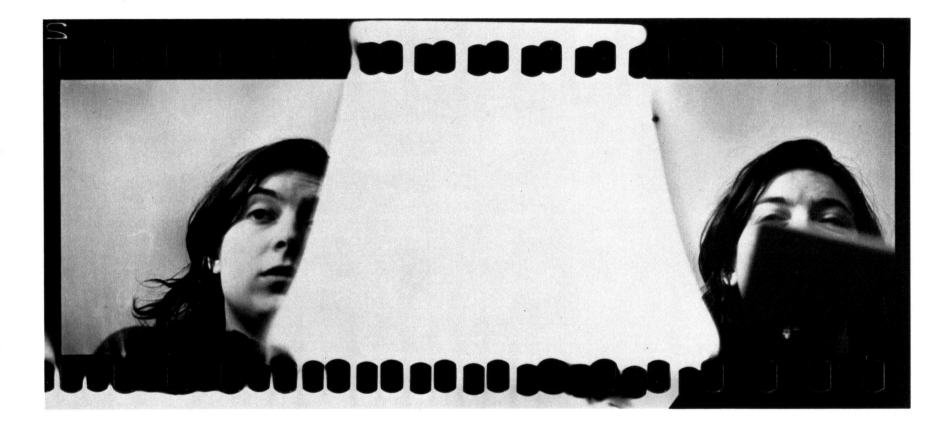

Mishaps in the darkroom can ruin pictures just as effectively as broken-down camera equipment. For the whole process of developing and printing a picture demands the delicate, exacting care needed for preparing a soufflé. Chemicals must be fresh and properly mixed or negatives turn out under- or overdeveloped; temperatures must be correct to make the emulsion produce a properly developed image; timing must be precise to ensure the proper degree of development. Even a slip in loading film onto a reel for development or insufficient agitation can ruin a picture *(above and opposite)*.

Darkroom disasters always show up on finished prints. White spots are a common flaw. They may be caused by dust or lint on the negative, and darkrooms should be kept as free of dust as possible—even walls should be wiped down regularly with a damp cloth. Dark splotches may result from air bubbles, which adhere to the surfaces of negatives when they are in the developer, thus preventing the chemicals from reaching the emulsion. Since air bubbles form in developer when film is being introduced, a tank should be tapped gently to eliminate them. Other defects, such as streaks and blank spots, can usually be traced to their sources with a little detective work.

A segment of totally undeveloped negative resulted when two parts of the film stuck together during the initial stage of development. The photographer's carelessness in winding the film onto the wire reel of his developing tank caused one loop of film to rest against the loop next to it, thus preventing the chemicals from reaching the emulsion at the area of contact.

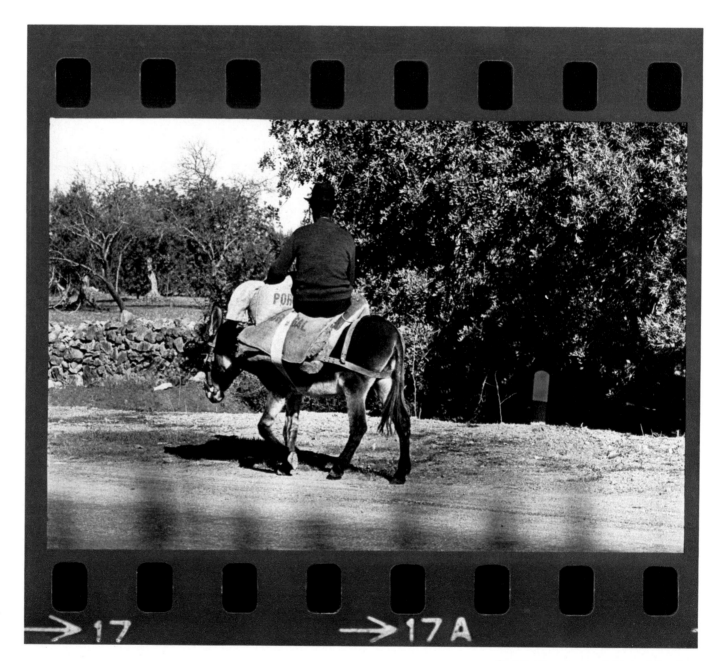

Dark streaks near sprocket holes (above) are caused by stale fixer and insufficient agitation of the developing tank. Enough fixer flowed through sprocket holes to halt development near the holes; but development continued on the rest of the negative.

Tracing Lines of Static

Professional photographers generally take pride in their talent for creating startling effects. But the bolt of lightning that appears to be striking the policeman on the sidelines *(right)* was a completely unpremeditated stroke—the chance effect of static electricity streaking across the film emulsion in the camera. The picture was taken at Yankee Stadium in New York during a game between the Giants and the Pittsburgh Steelers, on just the kind of crackling-cold, dry December day that causes sparks to jump between fingers and metal door handles—and, sometimes, from camera to film. The camera was a motorized Nikon that sped film through the camera at the rate of three frames a second, fast enough under cold, dry conditions to generate a sufficient charge for a spark.

Static electricity sometimes blights film in the darkroom. Pulling undeveloped film away from its paper backing too quickly can result in clusters of star-shaped static marks. Rubbing a hand along a strip of undeveloped film on a dry day may generate enough static to produce a row of black dots on the negative. It can sometimes be prevented from occurring in the camera simply by wiping the pressure plate with a solution of household detergent and water and permitting the plate to dry before loading the film. ☐

Catching the excitement of a Giants touchdown play, this shot registers dramatic currents that were not really there—a lightning flash caused by static electricity inside the camera.

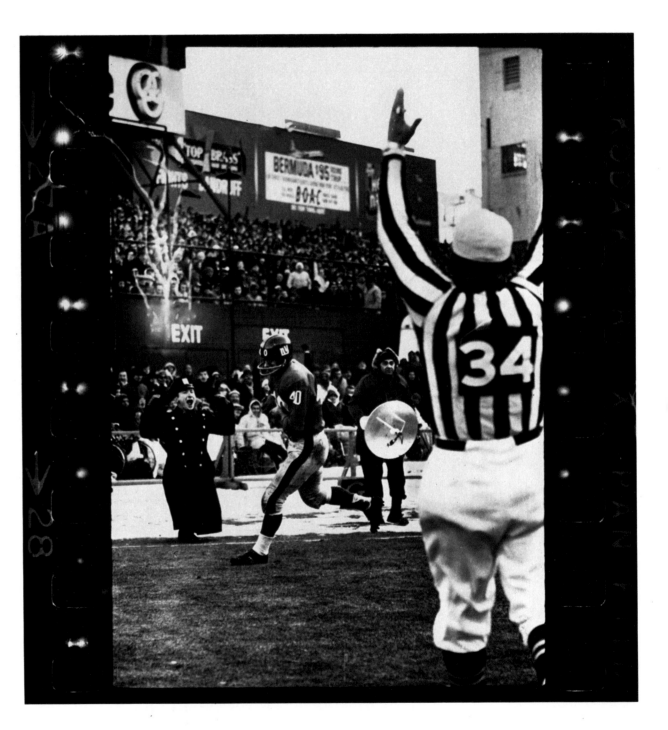

Photographing Action 5

Making a Still Picture Show Movement 128

Sports Photography—A Game without Rules 134
The Critical Instant 136
A Sequence to Show a Steal 138
Emphasizing Speed with Distortion 140
Freezing Action without Special Equipment 142
A Race Frozen by a Flash 144
Showing Motion with Background Blur 146
Panning at Perilous Speed 149
Obtaining New Views of Elusive Action 150
Suiting the Angle to the Sport 152
Zeroing In on a Race with a Zoom Lens 154

PHILLIP LEONIAN: *Man in Motion*, 1961

Making a Still Picture Show Movement

The businessman hurries along a busy New York City street, his stride wide, his briefcase swinging, his hat somehow remaining firmly on his head *(preceding page).* His gait tells us that he is in a rush. But to add to the sense of action, the photographer has allowed portions of the body to blur. Through this simple effect, a routine study of a walking man suddenly becomes an ingenious demonstration of motion portrayed on film.

All around are similar opportunities for making ordinary subject matter into extraordinary pictures by the simple expedient of conveying action. Few things in the real world stand still. Trees sway, children run and wrestle on the lawn, friends talk and gesticulate, traffic rushes by. Some situations are packed with action. Not just sports, although these provide great pictures for photographers—amateur as well as professional—who know how to get the shots that re-create a game's excitement. Though all kinds of events that are part of everyday life are photographed endlessly, too often they are photographed poorly because the action that animates them is missed. The tumult of a child's birthday party, a trip to an amusement park, a dance in the recreation room, a family picnic, a cocktail party—all are picture-making opportunities that call for special skill in conveying action if the pictures are to be more than routine.

One reason so many photographers fail to make the most of their opportunities to convey action is a mistaken belief that any kind of motion is the enemy of good photography. This prejudice is a hangover from the old days of slow film's bulky cameras and inadequate shutters. It seemed then that every other shot was marred by the blurred outlines of a squirming child or the suddenly turned head that fuzzed a smiling face. "Hold still," was the universal command from behind the camera. Such restriction is no longer necessary, for modern equipment does not demand rigid posing. The photographer who recognizes that fact and begins to seek and emphasize motion in his subjects will find a new dimension added to his picture making —but he will also find he has taken on a host of new problems. While they are varied, they all relate to one basic question: how can movement be shown in a photograph that does not move?

The answer to that question is simple and seemingly discouraging: it cannot be. No way has ever been found to record motion exactly the way the eye and brain perceive it. Even the pictures of movies and television do not move; they only seem to because of an optical illusion. The physical impossibility of recording motion has intrigued artists for many thousands of years, and they have worked out methods for conveying the idea of motion, if not the actual motion itself, in images—drawn, sculpted or photographed—that do not move. There are only three basic techniques:

1 | Freezing the action, with every detail clear and sharp, suggests that the

eye has caught a quick glimpse of an object, isolating one instant from a continuous flow of movement.

2 | A sequence of separate pictures conveys the pattern of movement, showing not one part of it but several parts as the motion progresses from beginning to end.

3 | Blurring, which appeared rather late in the history of art, conveys an impression of speed because the eye, too, sees rapidly moving objects—such as a spinning airplane propeller—as a blur.

A most dramatic way of portraying action in photographs is by freezing motion. This technique produces the most familiar of the action shots—the runner breasting the tape at the finish line, the woodchopper in mid-swing, the party jokester with his head thrown back, laughing at his own story. The faces are easily recognizable, the pictures are unmarked by blurs, and such movements as arm-waving are caught in mid-motion but are nevertheless sharp. This fidelity to detail contains one drawback—it somehow lessens the realism of the picture. The human eye cannot pick up such detail from figures in motion. The camera sees better than the eye, its super-reality adding an air of unreality. But because stop-action photographs pick out detail the eye would miss, they can often be stunning in their visual impact, presenting an entirely new perspective on the world.

It is easy enough to make stop-action pictures when a high-speed strobe unit or a fast shutter speed can be used. A small strobe gives a flash of light lasting only about 1/1000 second, an exposure short enough to freeze the most energetic child jumping on his bed. And many 35mm cameras also provide shutter speeds of 1/1000 second, fast enough under certain circumstances to stop a 60 mile-an-hour car. But when such brief exposures are impractical, and they often are for one reason or another, action can still be frozen by a number of different techniques.

One of the most useful ways of stopping motion is to catch the action at its peak. Then it seems to be in motion but is actually stationary, and it can be frozen with even the simplest equipment. A child at the high point on a swing or seesaw is at the peak of his action; he has moved as far as he can go in one direction and comes to a momentary halt before beginning to move again in the opposite direction. Peak action is part of any rhythmic movement—a dancer at the top of his leap, a golfer at the beginning of his stroke, a boy at the highest point of his jump over a fence. Shooting at that instant not only seems to freeze the action but also produces exciting pictures because it captures a high point, the precise moment when energy is about to be released as the motion reverses its pattern. The face of a child perched on a swing just before the downward arc begins is alight with eager anticipation. The diver and the pole vaulter at the top of their upward thrusts reveal in their expressions and body control the utter intensity of their efforts.

To achieve good peak-action pictures, the photographer must train himself to anticipate the elusive moment when motion comes to its fleeting halt. The open shutter and the peak action must coincide exactly. A shutter button pushed slightly too early or too late produces unwanted blurring. With practice, the photographer learns to press the button slightly before the peak action. This allows for the split second it takes for the brain to send the message to the finger and the added fraction of a second for the camera's mechanism to open the shutter.

There is no peak to catch, however, in many kinds of action—a running boy, for instance, or a speeding car. Yet such continuous motion can also be frozen with slow exposures and simple equipment. One technique that works in these cases depends on the angle of the camera and the relative distance from the subject.

The greater the distance between the lens and subject, the less the shutter speed demanded to stop action. This is because the farther the moving subject is from the camera, the smaller its image on the film and the less the image can move as the subject moves. From 25 feet, for example, the picture of a running child would be blurred if shot at a shutter speed of 1/125 second. But this same picture taken at the same speed from 50 feet away will show an unblurred child. Thus, doubling the shooting distance greatly increases the capacity of the camera to freeze action.

As important as distance from the subject is the angle from which the picture is being taken. At 25 feet, a car speeding at 60 miles per hour straight across the camera's view can be stopped only with a shutter speed of 1/1000 second or faster. A slower shutter would produce only a long blur. Yet the speeding car, if photographed from head on, could be captured sharp and clear with a shutter speed of only 1/250 second. When the car streaks across the camera's field, the image shifts from one side of the scene to the other creating the extreme blur of motion. From head on, or an angle up to about 45°, the car's image does not really move very much. Its motion is principally its fairly slight increase in size as it approaches. (Head-on shots, even of a car, are perfectly feasible and safe if made from a vantage point on a turn.)

When distance or angle cannot reduce image movement enough to stop fast action, turning the camera—panning—will do so. If the subject is kept continuously centered in the viewfinder by careful panning, its image will always stay in the same spot on the film and there will be no blurring. Panning is a fairly simple technique that becomes almost automatic if it is practiced regularly. The feet should be planted firmly on the ground to avoid jerking the camera, and the entire upper half of the photographer's torso should move from one side to the other, not the camera alone. The entire motion should have a flowing grace that keeps the subject exactly centered.

Panning produces pictures in which the subject appears sharp while the background is blurred; the subject is recognizable and the blur helps reinforce the illusion of motion. When used to freeze a running boy in the midst of his sprint, for example, the drama of stopped motion is retained while the blurred backdrop makes obvious the fact that the boy is actually running.

While a stop-action picture freezes a moment for the photographer, a series of such pictures can provide the history of an event. Sequence photographs, taken in rapid succession, can be made with almost any camera, even fairly simple ones, but they are easier to manage if the film-advance and shutter-cocking operations are combined in one device; or better yet, are entirely automatic. Several cartridge-load cameras, priced between $30 and $145, have spring-wind motor drives that advance the film automatically. Most 35mm cameras can be operated manually in rapid sequence, since only two steps are necessary: pressing the shutter release, then advancing the film and recocking the shutter with a single swing of a lever. Both the cartridge-load and 35mm cameras can take a picture every second.

Making a series of pictures works particularly well for photographs of children. A boy running across the lawn with the family dog, an act that may cover only a few seconds, becomes a study of youthful exuberance. Child portraits are easier to make this way, too, for the sitter can be allowed to move about as much as he wants while the camera clicks away. And few pictures of youngsters are more charming than a series that begins as a two-year-old tentatively digs a spoon into some cake and ends when his face is smeared with chocolate.

While stop-action and sequence pictures halt action for closer inspection, their very clarity may belie the sense of motion. To simulate a feeling of action, many photographers deliberately blur pictures by using relatively slow shutter speeds. The shot of the busy businessman *(page 127)* is an example of a deliberate blur. It was made with a Hasselblad at ½ second while the camera was panned. The panning kept some of the figure sharp while the slow shutter speed gave partial blurring. The picture of Jimmy Clark racing in his Lotus on page 148 is a similar example of deliberate blur. Only the lower portion of Clark's face is sharp. The rest is blurred. Yet the images of the car and driver are clearly distinguishable even though not graphically delineated, and a sense of hurtling speed is conveyed.

Deliberate blurring lends animation and excitement to any action picture. A bird coming in to land on a feeding tray can be stopped sharp with a shutter speed of 1/250 second—except for the wings, which will blur. When taking pictures of guests at a cocktail party or wedding reception, the photographer might want to show the faces clearly but blur waving arms and hands to convey the liveliness of the affair. This combination of frozen and blurred action can be achieved by slowing shutter speed and anticipating the moment when the guests are at their most active. For the best pictures, rehearsals may be necessary: the face of the hostess passing canapés, for example, should be recognizable, yet the arms and canapé tray might be blurred to show motion, and several tries may be needed to keep her head still while the tray moves.

Nowhere can a photographer find a better stage for action pictures than the playing fields of organized sport. The action is fast, colorful and played out close at hand, within full view. Few amateurs take advantage of this opportunity, although SPORTS ILLUSTRATED photographer Neil Leifer believes they could rival the professionals. To begin with they have more freedom to experiment, he points out, simply because they are unencumbered by assignments. This freedom enables them to shoot at will without the pressure of satisfying a picture editor or client.

One amateur who has become a weekend sports photographer is Robert Smith, an art director for a New York advertising agency. A lifelong camera buff, Smith began taking pictures of sports events at the high school near his home when his daughter, Wendy, became a cheerleader. He soon became intrigued with the potential of this special brand of action photography and began attending every football game the school played. The first problem he had to work out was getting onto the field, where he could shoot without interference from spectators. The solution was easy. He had already taken a number of good pictures of the team from the front row of spectators; he made enlargements of these photographs and left them at the coach's office. When Smith stopped by the athletic department the next week to promise more prints of future games, he found waiting for him warm thanks and a season pass admitting him to the sidelines.

For an amateur, Smith's photographic equipment is elaborate. He has a Nikon F with a zoom lens that goes from 80 to 250mm, which he uses about 80 per cent of the time at the games. Its wide range of focal length enables him to get full-figure shots of the players no matter where they are on the field. His other camera is a Nikkormat outfitted with a 300mm lens that he uses for long pass plays and kick returns. On sunny days he keeps both cameras loaded with ASA 400 film and set at 1/500 second and f/16. He is in search of clear, unblurred pictures, primarily so that the boys on the team can easily recognize themselves, or at least spot their numbers. For this reason he never blurs deliberately.

Good sports-action pictures require a feel for the game. Smith has learned enough about football—and has seen enough games—to sense where the action is going to be. He likes to roam along the edges of the field and behind the end zone, going where he expects the next flurry of activity to take place. When he senses a pass on a third down with eight yards to go, he stations himself about 20 or 30 yards from the line of scrimmage, hoping the pass will come his way. If it does, he usually kneels for his shot, for two reasons—to set the players against the uncluttered background of the sky, and to keep spectators behind him from screaming at him to sit down.

Like many photographers, Smith sometimes prefocuses his camera. With shutter speed and aperture preset at his preferred 1/500 and f/16, he focuses on a point where he thinks the action will be—the goal line, for example—and then shoots when the runner crosses the line. (Similarly, a photographer shooting a horse race might, before the start, focus on the starting gate, on the first turn, and on the finish line, marking each of the focus points with a grease pencil on his lens-focusing ring.) Smith does not hesitate to use all his film. Three or four good pictures from a roll of film is a respectable average in action photography. He sometimes photographs sequences and talks wistfully about a motor for his camera, an expensive battery-powered attachment that advances the film automatically for a very rapid series of shots. But Smith is a realistic man as well as an avid photographer. The cost of the motor (between $360 and $550) and the extra film it would use up would be prohibitive. "I have a son in college," he says. "If I brought home a motorized Nikon, my wife would kill me."

The differences between what professional photographers want from a sports event and a skilled amateur like Smith are not that great. Primarily, the professionals are always searching for the different shot, the unusual angle, the fresh approach. Walter Iooss Jr., a SPORTS ILLUSTRATED photographer, likes the challenge of sports photography "because it's all been done before." Therefore, the photographer's job is to restate what's been done before with insight and imagination. To do so, Iooss relies heavily on telephoto lenses, either a 400mm or an even longer 600mm, which he uses with a motorized Nikon. To hold these heavy lenses steady—essential because their long focal length exaggerates blur from camera movement—Iooss employs a unipod, a support that has only one leg. Iooss likes the mobility the unipod gives him, enabling him to swing his long lenses around the field so that he can train them quickly on the ever-shifting scenes of action. With his long lenses, Iooss can focus on one player, even on his facial expression, isolating him, or his small zone of action, from the playing field and the throngs of fans in the multi-tiered stadiums. So doing, Iooss—like many another professional and amateur today armed with knowledge, imagination and modern equipment—brings forth the many faces of action. ☐

Sports Photography – A Game without Rules

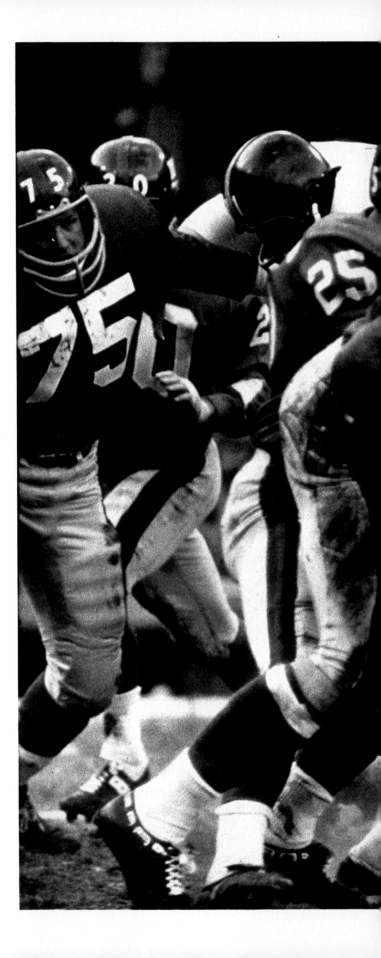

Motorists on a New York parkway one fall day in 1969 were dismayed to spot what looked like a radar speed-trap apparatus; drivers quickly throttled back to the speed limit of 60 mph. That was fine with the man behind the equipment, SPORTS ILLUSTRATED photographer Neil Leifer, for his rig was no radar but a special action camera, and to prepare it to photograph a downhill ski race that winter he needed a steady supply of 60 mph subjects. He had to adjust the movement of film running past a slit inside the camera until the film's motion exactly matched that of a car moving at the same speed, recording it clearly and sharply; then he knew he could get a similarly clear photograph of a similarly speeding skier *(page 146)*—whose downhill velocity also reached 60 mph, as he had found out by checking with the ski coach.

Elaborate preparations for one picture? Perhaps. But the photographer must know both the game and his equipment to capture the action of sport. No all-purpose rules work. Unusual pictures are made with gear like Leifer's, which makes a sharp picture of a moving object while blurring the background. But the basic camera-lens combinations many amateurs use every day can also convey the essence of a sport, by freezing movement at a crucial moment *(right),* catching action at its peak, or by introducing deliberate blur with panning. And some of the most exciting sports pictures are not single photographs but sequences showing the development of action.

If there is a single basic requirement for a good sports photograph, it is being in the right place at the right time. The crucial moments in sports are never repeated. No staging can ever recapture the action, the excitement and the color of an actual event; lost opportunities remain forever lost.

Rebuffed by the New York Giants' defense, Pittsburgh Steeler Theron Sapp (No. 33) is halted hard. This mad tangle was frozen at the moment of decision by SPORTS ILLUSTRATED photographer Walter Iooss Jr., who was set up on the sidelines with a 400mm lens on his motorized Nikon. The air of immediacy created by stopping players in mid-action is particularly successful for capturing the brutish grace of football: blurred figures lack definition and might leave the picture without a point.

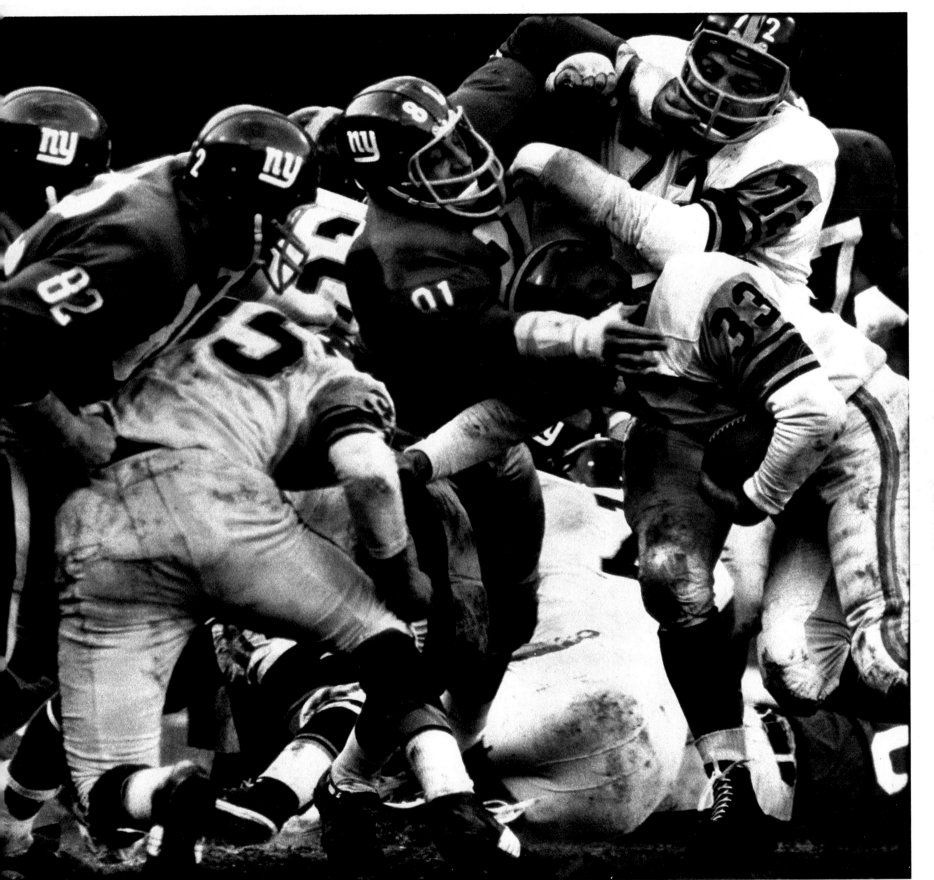

WALTER IOOSS JR.: *Giants' Defense*, 1963

135

The Critical Instant

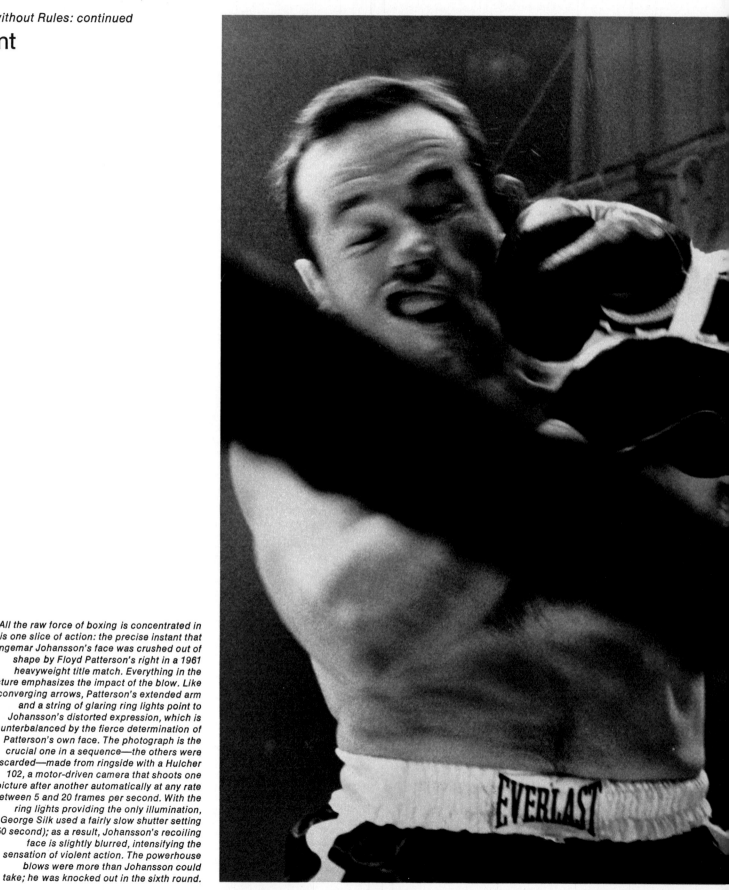

All the raw force of boxing is concentrated in this one slice of action: the precise instant that Ingemar Johansson's face was crushed out of shape by Floyd Patterson's right in a 1961 heavyweight title match. Everything in the picture emphasizes the impact of the blow. Like converging arrows, Patterson's extended arm and a string of glaring ring lights point to Johansson's distorted expression, which is counterbalanced by the fierce determination of Patterson's own face. The photograph is the crucial one in a sequence—the others were discarded—made from ringside with a Hulcher 102, a motor-driven camera that shoots one picture after another automatically at any rate between 5 and 20 frames per second. With the ring lights providing the only illumination, George Silk used a fairly slow shutter setting (1/150 second); as a result, Johansson's recoiling face is slightly blurred, intensifying the sensation of violent action. The powerhouse blows were more than Johansson could take; he was knocked out in the sixth round.

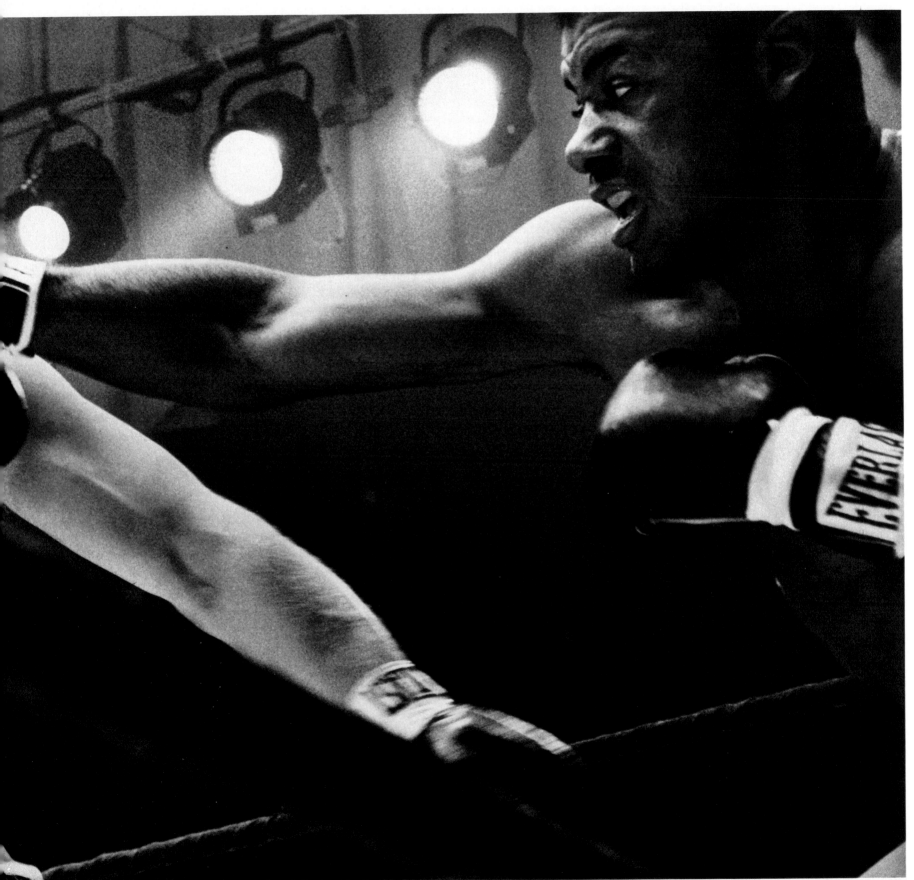

GEORGE SILK: *Johansson-Patterson Bout,* 1961

A Sequence to Show a Steal

1

2

3

4

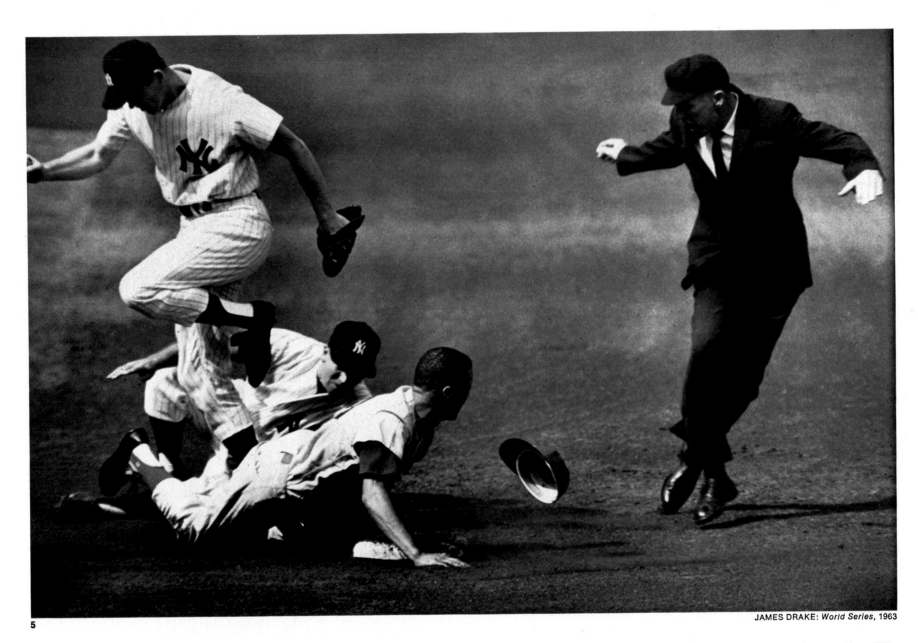

5

JAMES DRAKE: *World Series, 1963*

*Los Angeles Dodgers shortstop Maury Wills
safely steals second base in this sequence,
which tells the story of the play far better than a
single shot—the viewer can almost feel himself
sliding into second with Wills in the climactic
photograph above. Photographer James Drake,
high up in the press box at Yankee Stadium,
captured the action with a 1000mm lens.*

Emphasizing Speed with Distortion

United States trackmen taking a hurdle during tryouts for the 1960 Olympics seem to be racing even faster than they are because their figures are so weirdly elongated. George Silk made them look that way on purpose by an adjustment of a motorized slit camera that he helped design. Instead of setting the speed of its moving film strip to compensate for that of the action and thus freeze it totally, as is usually done, he ran the film slightly faster, stretching the runners' images on the film as it moved past the slit. A 200mm telephoto lens, used from a relatively short distance, created additional purposeful distortion; its flattening effect so compressed the runners that they appear to interlock in one hurtling mass.

Freezing Action without Special Equipment

The peak moment, that fleeting instant when an action reaches a high point and movement momentarily halts, is recorded at a Miami jai alai game as a player bounds into the air to snatch the ball off the wall. Since the action had come to this brief pause, a shutter speed of 1/250 second was sufficiently fast to freeze it.

A spring straight at the camera, stopped in mid-▶ air, powerfully conveys the dynamic energy of a collegiate broad jumper. Despite the speed of the action and only a relatively fast shutter setting—1/250 second—the image is unblurred. In a head-on view, there is little apparent motion of the subject, and it is easily frozen.

LYNN PELHAM: *Jai Alai Rebound,* 1965

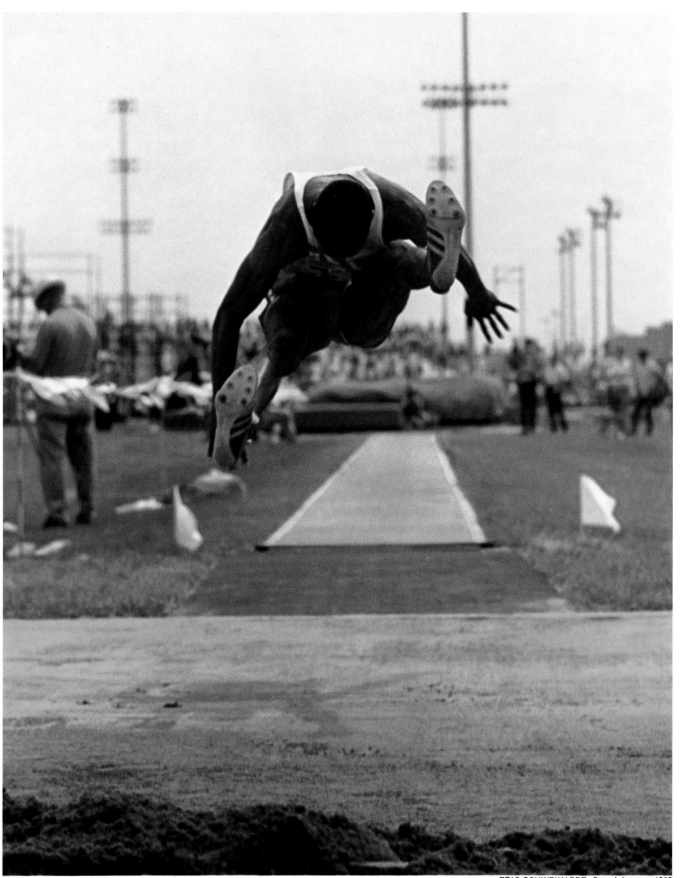

ERIC SCHWEIKARDT: *Broad Jumper,* 1969

A Race Frozen by a Flash

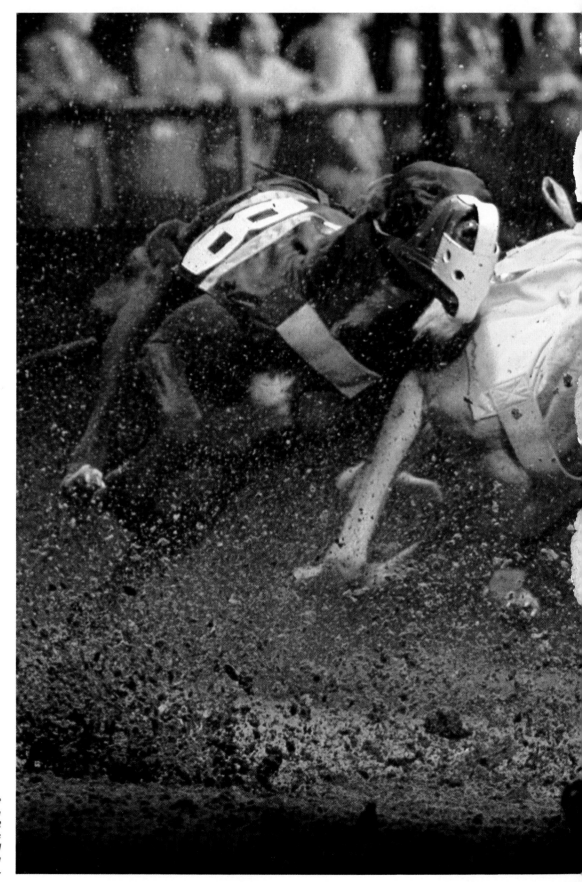

To dramatize the dirt-scattering frenzy of
greyhounds racing in Arizona, John Zimmerman
set up a bank of strobes over the track and shot
the hurtling dogs from ground level. The strobes
—flashed just after the front runner had passed
under the bank—momentarily froze the dogs in
frantic mid-air pursuit of the decoy rabbit.

JOHN ZIMMERMAN: *Greyhound Race,* 1962

Showing Motion with Background Blur

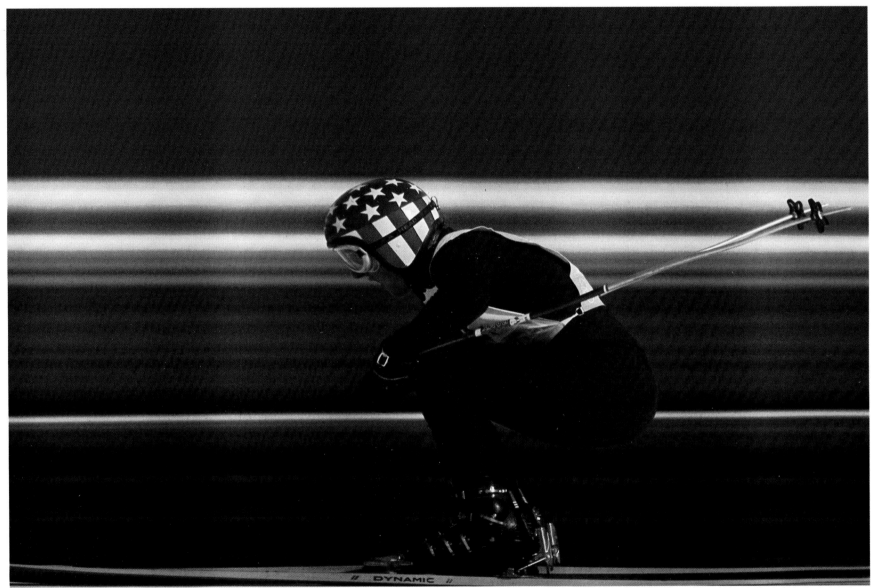

NEIL LEIFER: *Billy Kidd at Val Gardena, 1970*

*A Nikon equipped with a .004-inch slit shutter
and a motor-driven film strip was Neil Leifer's
solution to the problem of halting racer Billy
Kidd on an Italian slope. Leifer had time for only
two pictures, one of which is shown above, but
he succeeded in producing a startling
impression of speed as the moving film sharply
registered Kidd against the background blur.*

AL FRENI: *Bicycle Race*, 1969

Panning on the orange-shirted bicycle racer (left), Al Freni neatly isolated him from most of the other contenders, a blur behind his sharp figure. He was tracked in the viewfinder until he reached a spot upon which the camera had been focused in advance; at that moment, the shutter was released. A slow setting, 1/60 second, made the whirling spokes a silvery blur.

HORST BAUMANN: *The Lotus Winner*, 1963

148

*Only three feet separated Horst Baumann from
Jim Clark's Lotus as it sped to victory in
Britain's Grand Prix. At 100 mph, the car
produced the blurred image Baumann sought,
suggesting the excitement and pace of the sport.
He panned with Clark's head, making it slightly
sharper than the car hurtling past the
blurred background of the track. To heighten
the impression of speed Baumann used a
wide-angle lens; its tendency to exaggerate
foreground objects elongated the hood so that
the entire car seems to lunge forward.*

Obtaining New Views of Elusive Action

NEIL LEIFER: *Hawaiian Surf,* 1968

Patterns of foam and waves (above) were what Neil Leifer found when he took to a helicopter to photograph surfers on Waimea Bay, on the island of Oahu, in Hawaii. Shooting from above the action, he obtained not only a clear view of the surge and movement of a dangerous and hard-to-follow sport, but also an angle that lent itself to strong composition.

In photographing many a sport, the artistic challenge of conveying a sense of swift action may be outweighed by a more fundamental problem: getting close enough to show anything at all. The difficulty of getting within range is particularly acute in sports like surfing and sailing, where the moments of high drama—the riding of what might be the perfect wave, the turn of speed as a racing vessel's spinnaker fills—occur far from a photographer's usual van-

150

GEORGE SILK: *Surfers*, 1963

tage point, almost uncapturable from beach or dockside even by a man armed with such standard equipment as long lenses. But stunning pictures of such events can be obtained with special equipment that takes the camera to the athletes *(above and opposite).* And if the photographer knows where to place himself, even standard gear can bring fresh visual excitement to such frequently photographed sports as baseball and horse racing. ☐

While two surfers gracefully balance their boards off an Oahu beach, a third (far right) has already wiped out in this dramatic wide-angle view that photographer George Silk obtained while standing secure and dry on the shore. He bolted a plastic-housed motorized Nikon to the board at left and ran a string from the controls to the left hand of the surfer.

151

Suiting the Angle to the Sport

JAMES DRAKE: *Denny McLain at Work*, 1968

Denny McLain's ball is stopped in mid-air in this Detroit Tigers-Cleveland Indians game. James Drake used a long 600mm lens to project himself—and the viewer—from his position far behind the batter and plate umpire (at right) directly into the action. The blurred figures frame McLain and direct the eye to the ball.

After sunrise, George Silk took up a 3 a.m. dare and had himself hoisted in a boatswain's chair to the top of the aluminum mast of the 12-meter Nefertiti to capture this bird's-eye view. He used a wide-angle lens on his Nikon SP, pointing it downward at arm's length to bring the ballooning spinnaker into the picture.

GEORGE SILK: *Nefertiti,* 1962

Zeroing In on a Race with a Zoom Lens

WALTER D. OSBORNE: *Starting Gate at Aqueduct*, 1964

Walter Osborne's camera position—adjacent to the starting gate—made it easy to cover horse-race action with a normal lens. However, by using an 85-250mm zoom lens set near 250mm, he was able to compress the strung-out field of thoroughbreds, blur the action slightly and vividly convey the excitement and silken colors of a breakaway start at New York's Aqueduct.

The Assigned Problem 6

Photography in the Classroom 158
A Wealth of Facilities for Learning 160

Problems That Teach 162
New Light on the Common Egg 164
Private Views of a New Environment 166
Reflections through the Camera's Eye 168
Exploring the Effects of Movement 170
From Three Dimensions, A Flat Design 172

BILL EPPRIDGE: *Student Photographer at the Rochester Institute of Technology*, 1970

Photography in the Classroom

Today more and more people are finding out how to solve the problems of photography not by the haphazard process of trial and error but by going to school. In the past most young photographers perforce learned by doing, for only a sprinkling of American colleges and technical institutions considered photography an appropriate subject for study. "There was no place I could go . . . for photographic education," wrote Ansel Adams of his efforts in the 1920s to master the art of landscape photography. "Excepting the few kind individuals who provided assistance, and some nuts-and-bolts training in photofinishing shops, I trained myself—very inefficient!" To help aspiring young photographers avoid the frustrations he himself experienced, Adams has conducted a photographic workshop in Yosemite, California. In doing so, he contributes to a growing national phenomenon.

According to a survey conducted in 1968 by a member of the Department of Printing and Photography at Southern Illinois University, the number of United States colleges and universities that offer some instruction in photography had increased by two thirds in the previous four years, and the number of students had almost doubled, increasing from 14,000 to 26,000. By 1970, photography could be studied as a college course in 440 schools, and 48 of them offered bachelor's degrees for a major in photography. The range of subject matter taught in formal classes is very broad. Courses range from elementary introductions to picture taking and processing, through advanced seminars in photographic history, and on to such specialties as photography for television, medicine and law.

Photography is the major concern of a number of specialized private institutes and nondegree schools, where intensive training in photographic art and techniques is offered without the liberal arts courses that accompany most college programs. The institutions offering bachelor's degrees generally place photographic classes either in the journalism or art departments. Only seven have independent photography departments. Foremost of these is the School of Photographic Arts and Sciences, part of the Rochester Institute of Technology, which is located in upstate New York. The Institute, founded in 1829 when Rochester was a frontier farming community, is an enormous complex of science, business and arts colleges housed on a 1,300-acre campus of modern, brick buildings on the outskirts of Rochester. The Photography School is one of the Institute's major entities and offers a greater variety of photography courses—38 in all—than any other institution in the country, and confers both a Bachelor of Fine Arts and a Bachelor of Science degree.

Like other students at the Institute, those in the School of Photography tend to concentrate on the practical—understandably. Rochester is an industrial town, and one of the best places in the world to earn a living in

The campus of Rochester Institute of Technology, completed in 1968, includes seven different colleges, as well as libraries, athletic facilities and a student housing complex. This view from the top of the College of Graphic Arts and Photography shows the College of General Studies (left) and the James E. Booth Memorial Building of Fine and Applied Arts.

photography. Photography is in the air. It was here that George Eastman in 1888 began manufacturing the simple box camera that expanded picture taking from the hobby of a dedicated few into a national craze. It is here that the Eastman Kodak Company, now the world's largest manufacturer of cameras and film, still maintains its headquarters. Kodak lends close support to the photography school. It provides guest lecturers, occasionally offers advice on the curriculum, opens its libraries and gives technical advice to students working on special projects—and hires many of them when they complete their education.

Partly because of this industrial backing, R.I.T. has the most elaborate facilities in the country. It is the only school to educate students for degrees in a technological specialty called Photographic Science and Instrumentation, turning out engineers who design new cameras, concoct new kinds of film and develop the complex photographic equipment used in many branches of scientific research. The even more specialized Department of Bio-Medical Photography offers the country's only collegiate program in the techniques of photographing living organisms for scientific research.

Most of R.I.T.'s 860 photography students are concentrating on becoming well-rounded professional photographers. "We are preparing young people for meaningful jobs," explains the school's director, William S. Shoemaker. In addition to basic classes in picture taking and laboratory techniques, the students can choose from elective courses in portraiture, advertising photography, photojournalism and motion-picture photography. One major program in professional photography, leading to a Bachelor of Science, includes training in business management and accounting for students who plan to enter industry or to open their own studios. Another program concentrates on esthetics, and leads to the fine arts degree. In both, the emphasis is on learning by doing. From virtually the first day of class, students are assigned challenging photographic problems, and sent out of class to solve them. The result of this guided do-it-yourself approach, Shoemaker hopes, will be a highly developed sixth sense of "visual literacy"—the ability to think and communicate in photographic images. He sums up the goals of the Rochester school by saying, "We're trying to provide educational experiences that will teach young people to solve the problems of visual communication."

A Wealth of Facilities for Learning

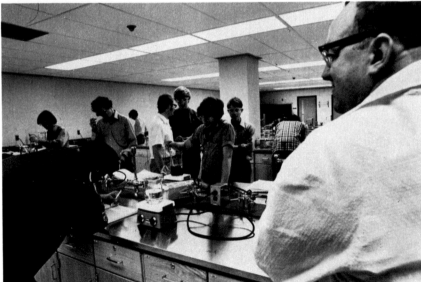

R.I.T.'s School of Photography is one of the few places where a student can learn how to develop film in an automatic Versamat Film Processor—or how to use a Video Color Negative Analyzer to gauge the proper color values for making a good print *(opposite, top right).* Such highly specialized machines are part of a two-million-dollar inventory of photographic equipment.

Housed in a massive red brick building that it shares with the Institute's School of Printing, the photography school provides fully equipped movie studios and a sound stage, still-photography studios, and processing laboratories for both black-and-white and color work. All together, the school has 172 darkrooms. Chemicals for processing film are mixed in waist-high, 250-gallon vats in a special room; 150 gallons of fixer alone must be prepared every day to fill the school's needs. Aside from the equipment available in still- and motion-picture studios, students can execute assignments by choosing from among 340 cameras, including 57 view cameras and 52 movie cameras, as well as a variety of lenses, strobe units, tripods and filters. As many as 1,000 separate items may be issued to students on a busy day. □

Preparing a supply of paper developer (top), extension student Gary Morse pours commercially blended chemicals into a vat in the Chemical Mixing room. Freshman students in the chemistry lab (bottom) learn to blend their own developers. In this experiment, they are required to eliminate one of the ingredients to discover the effect on processed negatives.

The inverted image of a chocolate cake on the screen of a studio view camera (top left) shows a student's effort to compose a still life. At top right, a teacher uses a color-negative analyzer to point out color values in a transparency to junior Denny Harrod. Freshman

Cary Keshen (bottom left) adjusts his view camera to photograph the futuristic skylights atop a campus building. In a color-printing darkroom (bottom right), sophomore Irving Baker inspects a strip of 35mm negatives before putting it into the enlarger at his left.

Problems That Teach

A former member of the R.I.T. faculty, Ralph Hattersley, once compared the teaching of photography with the classic tale of the blind men trying to describe an elephant. One man, who had taken hold of the elephant's tail, maintained the animal was long and slithery, like a snake. Another ran his fingers over the animal's leg and insisted that an elephant is a huge, wrinkled cylinder, like the trunk of a giant tree. Such is the case with photography, Hattersley maintains. The field has grown so gigantic and complex that no one can grasp all of it, and photography teachers must grope their way. "We have lost our main means for determining what goals our students should pursue," Hattersley wrote. "How can we know what to teach them?"

The faculty at R.I.T. solves this predicament by teaching the students to deal creatively with challenge. "Photographic assignments are treated as special problems; we try to give the students sufficient technical background so that they can solve the problems they will confront," says Tom Wilson, staff chairman of the school's Photographic Illustration Department.

Sometimes the problems are purely technical. How do you arrange the lighting for a strong, effective portrait? What kind of camera do you choose, what film, what developing and printing methods? R.I.T. students are bombarded with technical information on strobe lights, umbrella reflectors, developing compounds and printing tricks.

But in most of the problems that students are asked to solve, technique merges into interpretation. The picture of a halved cabbage on the opposite page resulted from an assignment to produce a high-quality print using one of various lab techniques taught in the freshman introductory course. By emphasizing contrast, Hugh Barton transformed the image of a rather humble vegetable into a photographic design of singular beauty and originality.

The problems are even more challenging in the upper-class courses. One instructor assigned his second-year students to photograph any ordinary object—a water glass, a lamppost, a piece of Swiss cheese—and, by means of lighting and composition, give it an aspect of monumentality. Another posed the following problem to his seniors: "I am an art director. I need a photograph which is based on the theme 'The Good Old Days.' Its tone may be sentimental, nostalgic, ironic, playful, sad, silly, somber. Its content is up to you." And still another teacher, who began his course by having students shoot pictures of sugar cubes, ended it by asking them to indicate photographically their attitudes toward such sweeping concepts as death, sex and man's inhumanity toward man.

Assigned to produce "a print of outstanding ▶ merit," freshman Hugh Barton picked a seemingly commonplace subject, a red cabbage sliced in half, which he photographed on Plus-X film with a 4 x 5 view camera. He printed on high-contrast paper to convert the image of the folded leaves to a powerful, convoluted design.

HUGH G. BARTON: *Red Cabbage*, 1970

New Light on the Common Egg

KAREN KELLERHOUSE: *Texture*, 1970

JOHN McQUADE: *Illusion*, 1969

No object seems more ordinary than a hen's egg. That is precisely why several classes of R.I.T. students were assigned to take pictures of eggs—to test their ability to show a mundane subject in an unusual way. The students, using different lighting and darkroom techniques, plus a liberal amount of imagination, made some extraordinarily varied statements about the properties of eggs. One focused a pencil-thin spot-

light on a small part of the shell *(above, left),* creating a sense of texture that seems as warm and palpable as human skin. Another demonstrated the basic geometry of eggs *(opposite, top left),* photographing them from above in natural light and printing for maximum contrast to eliminate every quality besides shape. Still others *(opposite, bottom row)* seem to comment on the properties of light itself.

The precarious balance in the picture above is actually an illusion. The eggs were placed next to a piece of black cardboard on a glass pane, lighted from below and photographed from above. At left above, a spotlight reveals surprising texture in a supposedly smooth egg.

High-contrast printing turned eggs into circles ▶ of white space (opposite, 1). A tiny light beam aimed at each end of the hollowed-out shell in the foreground made it glow with a light of its own (2). A pattern of light streaks was thrown onto these eggs from a spotlight with a special lens (3). Two eggs are silhouetted against the large spherical disk of a floodlight reflector (4).

1   GREG HULJACK: *Geometric Pattern*, 1969

2   KEITH HUNT: *Inner Glow*, 1970

3   JONATHAN HASKELL: *Lightstruck*, 1969

4   JONATHAN HASKELL: *Silhouettes*, 1969

Private Views of a New Environment

DENNIS KRUKOWSKI: *Midnight Mist, 1970*

One of the first tasks that many teachers set for their freshman classes is to photograph the campus—not just as a collection of buildings, but as an environment. "R.I.T. offers you a new realm of experiences," counseled one instructor. "How you perceive, interpret and record these experiences is the essence of this project." The instructor suggested three approaches. Students could look for a way to express the clean, functional style of campus architecture. Or they could treat the assignment as a problem in photojournalism and show other students adapting to the recently built campus. Finally, they might try to extend their vision into the realm of surrealism and convey a personal image of the campus in any form their imagination conceived—the approach adopted by two students whose photographs are shown here.

A somber disquiet pervades this time exposure, made at night in a heavy fog, of lights and pathways receding into nowhere. The off-focus silhouette of the bicycle looms menacingly above the eye of the camera, which was placed on the ground; yet the bicycle also adds an odd human element to the seemingly vacant campus.

Stark black shapes silhouetted against the ▶ failing light of an evening sky give a strange emphasis to the modernistic lines of the R.I.T. campus. "I was purposely looking for a high-contrast effect, as this was my impression of the campus," says Jim Barstow, the student. "By overexposing and underdeveloping, I was able to catch the scene as I saw it."

JIM BARSTOW: *Dusk*, 1970

Reflections through the Camera's Eye

DONALD SCHELLER: *London, 1970*

Reflections—in windowpanes, in mirrors, in the shining surfaces of automobile bodies, vending machines and other metallic objects—are an important part of every photographer's visual vocabulary. Used effectively as an integral part of a picture's composition they lend sparkle and surprise to an otherwise ordinary subject. Sometimes the reflection itself may become the subject of a picture.

Many R.I.T. teachers send their students into the field with the specific problem of photographing reflections. The picture on the bottom of the opposite page is the result of one such field trip. In asking a junior class to take photographs in which reflections provide the center of interest, Visiting Lecturer Derek Drage also warned against one of reflection's major hazards—destroying a picture's clarity and strength by making it too complex.

R.I.T. students often use reflections to enhance the pictures they take outside of class assignments *(top, opposite)*. And one sophomore, while photographing a street scene on a trip to London, developed on his own a bit of camera legerdemain for creating the appearance of a mirror image *(above)* where almost no reflections existed.

The reflections in this looking-glass world are out-and-out fakes, produced by an intentional double exposure. Donald Scheller aimed his camera out the plate-glass window of a London café, and caught a young mother standing by a baby carriage and eating an ice-cream cone. He then advanced his film a half frame, waited until the woman moved to the other side of the carriage and shot again. The second exposure overlapped the first and created an odd image that looks like—and yet unlike—a mirror reflection.

By asking a young boy to hold up a mirror in front of his face (right, top), third-year student Garry Thall put reflections to work photographically in an unusual way, and at the same time created a visual metaphor for what he describes as a "headless, nonthinking society." The picture was taken while driving through the Rochester environs with another junior, Mark Hockman, who had been given a class assignment to photograph reflections. Hockman came up with a picture within a picture (bottom)—the reflected images of passersby in the polished metal cover of an ice machine on the sidewalk of a small country town.

GARRY THALL: *Faceless Boy*, 1970

MARK HOCKMAN: *Scottsville, New York*, 1970

Exploring the Effects of Movement

One problem photographers must face repeatedly is the difficulty of showing movement in a still photograph *(pages 127-133)*. To help students develop expertise in solving this basic dilemma, instructors frequently ask their classes to explore various motion-conveying techniques, such as panning, blurring and high-speed photography. As a result, these techniques become such an instinctive part of a student's repertoire that he uses them to create not only a sense of motion, but a wide range of additional effects.

Both of the pictures on this page use blurred motion to enhance a mood. But one was made by keeping the camera stationary while the subject moved, thus producing a ghostlike image that seems to float along a murky corridor *(left)*. The other added excitement to a stationary subject *(opposite)* with deliberate camera motion.

Blurry outlines, hazy lighting and calculated distortion all add an otherworldly quality to this one-second time exposure. Freshman Dennis Early asked the model, Mrs. Early, to wear a hip-length blouse, and told her to pivot on her right foot during the exposure, thus blurring the outlines of her left arm and leg. To dematerialize the scene further, he distorted perspective by tilting the adjustable back of his 4 x 5 view camera; this made the narrow corridor walls slope outward slightly as they rise from the darkness at their base toward the only light source, a bare bulb in the ceiling fixture.

DENNIS A. EARLY: *Apparition,* 1970

Assigned to take a photograph that would "convey a sense of the action of today's swinging generation," third-year student Charles Kirman produced this vibrant portrait. Though the model is standing still, Kirman charged his picture with vitality and movement by pivoting his 35mm camera up and down during the ¼-second exposure. In addition, he deliberately upset the equilibrium of the picture by choosing a high camera angle that seems to throw the model slightly off balance, as though she were about to take a forward step. The result was so successful that Kirman was able to sell the photograph to a local newspaper.

CHARLES KIRMAN: *Woodland Girl,* 1970

From Three Dimensions, a Flat Design

The distinguishing talent of Edward Weston, one of the masters of photography, was his ability to picture ordinary objects in such a way that their qualities of form and shape were emphasized, but the object itself remained recognizable. One of Weston's most famous pictures is a close-up of a ceramic toilet bowl he photographed from below to give it an odd sense of monumentality. The same utilitarian item, treated in a somewhat different way, was picked by R.I.T. freshman Judie Gleason for her own study in transforming normal appearances.

Miss Gleason's assignment was to photograph any three-dimensional object in such a way "as to reduce the illusion of three-dimensionality as much as possible," thus creating a flat pattern of light and dark shapes. At the same time, the object itself would have to retain its identity.

There is no mistaking the object Miss Gleason chose. Yet by a wise selection of visual design elements—a squarely overhead camera angle, careful framing and strong contrast of black and white—she has in effect created an optical illusion in which the solid toilet bowl seems almost as flat as the tile floor it rests on. □

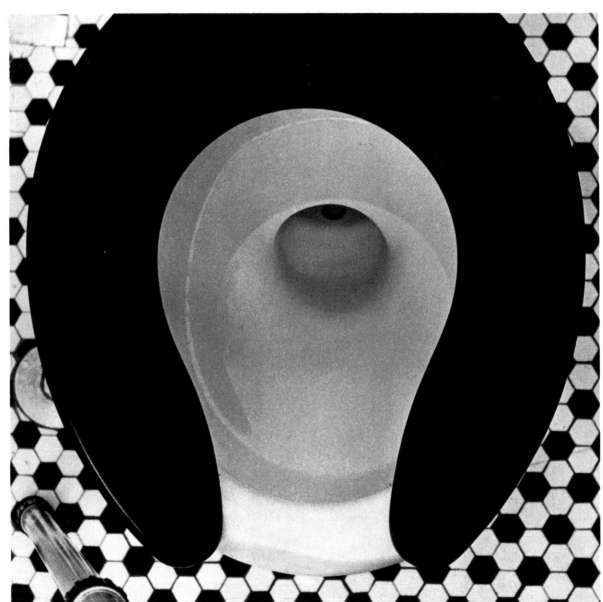

JUDIE GLEASON: *Toilet Bowl,* 1967

The main visual clue that lets the eye recognize three dimensions is gradation in shading between light and dark. By including a minimum of gray tones in this view of a toilet bowl, Miss Gleason has produced a strongly two-dimensional pattern of black and white.

The Deliberate Mistake 7

How to Succeed by Breaking the Rules 176

Using Graininess to Make the Particular General 178

Stark Black and White for Emotional Power 180

Shadows to Startle the Eye 182

Drama from the Misused Film 184

Making a Point by Chopping Off Heads 186

The Power of Distorted Perspective 188

Tampering with Lenses to Break Up the Light 190

For Mystery, Focus on the Wrong Thing 192

Mellow Tints from Reciprocity Failure 194

Sun Shots to Turn Day into Night 196

Sacrificing Detail to Create a Mood 198

An Inferior Lens for Superior Effects 200

Indoor Film to Create a New View of the Outdoor World 202

Hardly anybody ever takes a picture of a boy fishing by shooting his bare feet. But the choice of a bizarre angle to do what nobody does, consciously refusing to accept ordinary rules, gave this picture its impact. It was taken at high noon on a bright summer day on Lake Washington near Seattle, with the camera aimed upward from under the fishing pier. Exposure calculated for the sky underexposed and darkened the silhouetted foreground objects.

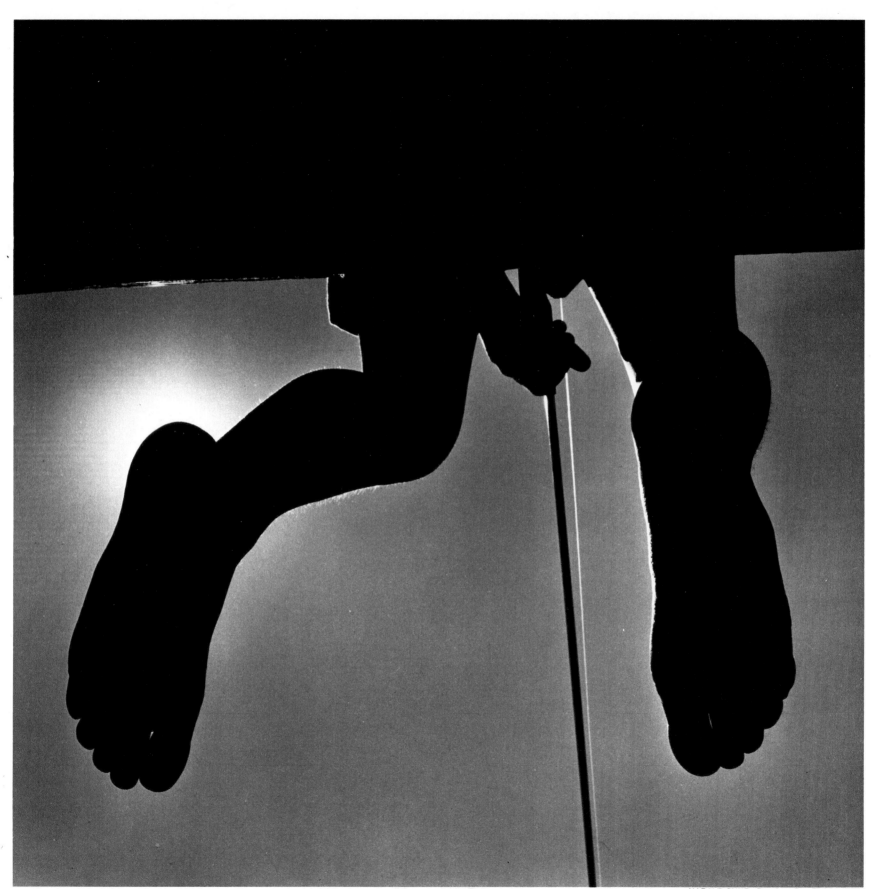

HARALD SUND: *Barefoot Boy Fishing*, 1967

How to Succeed by Breaking the Rules

It gets harder and harder to break the rules of picture taking accidentally, because so much photographic equipment is being designed to prevent mistakes that might mar the final print. For instance, it is impossible to make double exposures with some of today's cameras; on most, the mechanism that cocks the shutter is constructed to advance the film simultaneously, inextricably tying the two functions together and ensuring a fresh frame for every exposure—so long as the film is loaded correctly. Very fast film, which could once be relied on to produce the overall mottling of graininess, is today so formulated that it combines its great sensitivity to light with freedom from excessive graininess in the final print or transparency.

If a photographer has reached the stage of wanting to express himself freely, perhaps by seeking, for effect, results that ordinarily are avoided, he might seem frustrated by the improvements photochemists and engineers have labored to produce. Their success imposes limitations on the mistakes he can make. To thwart him further, few manuals include instructions on how to achieve other than the correct results in photography. But ingenious souls among the photographic fraternity continue to dream up unusual practices to create striking pictures. Actually, the great proliferation of new kinds of equipment makes it easier to experiment with unorthodox techniques. Occasionally an unusual method is discovered by sheer accident (as Lilo Raymond did when she produced the picture at right), but most are employed on purpose by photographers seeking to give their work graphic originality or to underscore its emotional content.

If a photographer wants to make multiple images, there are several ways he can double expose his film. On some cameras, the device that prevents double exposures can be disconnected *(pages 114-115).* And even cameras lacking such an override can be manipulated to keep the film from moving as the shutter is cocked. With most 35mm single-lens reflex cameras, the following procedure will work. After making the first exposure, hold the rewind crank with the left hand to keep the film from advancing; then press in on the rewind button with the little finger of the right hand, and use the right thumb to operate the film-advance lever. This will cock the shutter, making possible a second exposure on the stationary film. A more elaborate technique involves rewinding the film into its cassette (being careful to leave the end protruding), then putting the film through the camera a second or third time; it is necessary to take pains to align the sprocket holes in the same relative position to get exposures in good register.

When using any of these multiple-exposure methods, be sure to allow for the extra light that will reach the film; underexpose each of the overlapped pictures by one or two f-stops, depending on how many shots are combined. (Of course, multiple images may easily be made in the darkroom, either by

To shoot some pictures of children staging a make-believe parade, Lilo Raymond used orthodox equipment—a 35mm camera with a 50mm lens; and technique—she exposed at f/8 for 1/125 second. The rule she broke belongs more to the housewife's code than the photographer's: always empty the pockets of any garment headed for the washing machine. When she put her jeans into the laundry, Miss Raymond forgot to take the finished roll of film out of one pocket. And a washed, rinsed and dried roll came out with the washed, rinsed and dried jeans. Miss Raymond "was heartbroken—I knew the roll would have been good—but I decided to process it anyway." This proved difficult, what with layers of film sticking to each other and the emulsion cracking and peeling in spots, but in the end it was all worthwhile: a zebra-stripe pattern formed a delicate tracery across each picture and served to frame the children like figures in a fantasy landscape.

LILO RAYMOND: *Children Playing,* 1968

combining two or more negatives into a "sandwich" before enlarging them or by enlarging them one after the other onto the same piece of printing paper. Many photographers, however, prefer to create their effects on a single negative, working entirely with the camera.)

Special efforts are needed even to create the image distortions that inadequate lenses caused in the camera's early years. Various methods will serve. Shooting through raindrops on a window is a favorite way of achieving distortion and since any highly polished curved surface reflects a distorted image, it too can be used to get the effect. Often it is possible to photograph a reflection of the subject in the chrome trim of a car—a bumper, a wheel cover, even the bright strip around a headlight. As simple a device as a large sheet of heavy-duty aluminum foil gives a surprisingly clear reflection, which can be contorted into any desired form by twisting the foil. But, because the reflected image lies not on the same plane as the reflecting surface but behind the reflector, focusing on the reflector may leave the reflection blurred, and vice versa *(pages 54-55).* In order to get equally clear images of reflection and reflector, the lens must usually be stopped down to increase depth of field and keep all planes in sharp focus.

Unlike distorted images and double exposures, a few other kinds of mistakes are now easier to make on purpose because they depend on equipment and materials not generally available in the old days. Perspective, for example, can be distorted by using an ordinary wide-angle lens. It will overemphasize near objects at the expense of far ones: If a little girl is seated on the ground holding her doll out to the camera, a wide-angle lens can make the doll seem a gargantuan monster held by a puppet-sized child, achieving this effect through the lens's exaggeration of size differences that are normally associated with distance. To get the depth of field needed to keep both foreground and background sharp, the aperture should be closed down and the camera focused on a point a little nearer the camera than the mid-point between foreground and background.

The photographer who puts his mind to it will find many ways to do things wrong in order to get the right picture. Even such a seemingly simple technique as deliberate underexposure is subject to a number of variations, each producing different effects—harsh contrasts, silhouettes, extreme graininess. Filters, altering shades of gray in black-and-white pictures, can make a blue sky black or a ruddy complexion pale. Ignoring the recommendations for color film use can turn hues topsy-turvy or render a colorful scene in monochrome. But whatever the technique adopted, rules are broken at the breaker's peril. They exist because, in most cases, they are necessary. Successful violations generally depend on knowing in advance the effect that is wanted, rather than on random, trusting-to-luck trials.

Using Graininess to Make the Particular General

Graininess—or the mottled appearance caused by the uneven clumping of silver particles in the negative image—was seldom a problem in the old days of photography, much less a pictorial effect to be sought deliberately. Most cameras used large plates, which produced quite big pictures that did not have to be enlarged. Although the silver clumps were present, they were too small to be obvious in contact prints.

Photographers began to worry about graininess (and to capitalize on its potential usefulness) only after they had switched to small, fast films—35mm and 2¼ x 2¼—that require great enlargement, particularly if only part of a negative is to be printed. Fast film contains large grains of silver; even slight clumping of these particles becomes noticeable in an enlargement, roughening the texture of the photograph and obliterating its details. These defects can be avoided in pictures taken and processed under carefully controlled conditions, but they came to be accepted in journalistic photographs—and even admired for the atmosphere they conveyed, suggesting a dramatic event recorded at a crucial moment. On occasion this effect was imitated, and graininess was deliberately introduced in an attempt to inject an air of synthetic excitement into an ordinary photograph. But graininess can lend other qualities to a picture. Manipulated by a talented photographer, its texture and its masking of detail can so simplify a scene that the basic elements gain additional power. In the picture at right, graininess has transformed a view of two boys and their dog into a broad comment on childhood.

The techniques used for encouraging graininess are the same as those that encourage an emulsion to respond to the least amount of light, for the larger the size of the crystals, the larger the resulting clumps of silver. Thus fast films generally produce grainier negatives than slow ones. Graininess can be increased by overdevelopment, which forces crystals that have been only slightly affected during exposure to turn into silver, and "burning in" a densely exposed part of a negative can also accentuate graininess in the enlargement. And of course great enlargement makes graininess obvious, so magnifying the negative that the resulting picture emerges with a rough texture that softens details.

A young Seattle photographer named Harald Sund, who admires the ability of children to be "alone but not lonely," tried to capture the self-contained tranquility of two boys and their dog on a hilltop near the end of a summer day. Since he meant to comment on the nature of childhood rather than to make a study of specific youngsters, Sund set his Bronica low—on the grass below the crest of the hill, silhouetting tree and figures against the sky. He then reduced detail further by making his picture as grainy as possible. He used a fast (ASA 400) film, blew up only a third of the 2¼ x 2¼ negative, and burned in the top portion of the print for an extra few seconds. This additional exposure darkened the sky area enough to prevent it from being a stark white space, making it a mottled gray to counterbalance the solid black of the silhouetted tree and figures.

HARALD SUND: *Childhood*, 1967

179

Stark Black and White for Emotional Power

One of the marks of the great photograph has always been a great range of tone—the maximum number of subtle shades of gray, delineating detail in exquisite precision. And yet some subjects are best rendered in solid blacks and whites with few gray shades between. In these harshly unequivocal tones almost all detail is lost, but the very lack supplies raw force to a grotesque natural form such as a weirdly gnarled tree, or to a tense street scene like the one at right.

The stark black-and-white effect is achieved by deliberately exaggerating the contrast of negative or print or both together. Some materials are specifically designed to increase contrast. The copy film used to shoot the portraits on pages 184-185, for example, is a high-contrast film. (A low-contrast print may be copied on it to increase contrastiness.) There are high-contrast developers, such as Kodak D-19 or Agfa 40. And printing papers are available in many grades of contrast.

A good technique for getting high contrast is to underexpose the film and then overdevelop it. With underexposure, comparatively few crystals in the emulsion are affected by light; these are completely converted to silver by overdevelopment to provide the print's blank whites, while the unaffected areas of the emulsion remain empty to provide the print's solid blacks. Raising the temperature of the developer solution above the level recommended by its manufacturer makes its action more rapid and produces overdevelopment in a conveniently short period of time. This is the method Peter deFrancis used to get the high contrast shown in the picture at right.

A nighttime demonstration in Washington, D.C., held in 1970 after a fatal confrontation between students and National Guard at Ohio's Kent State University, was a high-key subject whose drama seemed best rendered in the bold blacks and whites of high contrast. To achieve maximum contrastiness, photographer Peter deFrancis, who uses only his last name professionally, employed a very high-speed film but exposed for only 1/60 second at f/2.8 —about a fourth as much as the meter reading called for. He then exaggerated the effects of underexposure by overdeveloping the film. According to the manufacturer's guide, developing at 68°F. for eight minutes would give normal contrast. But deFrancis went beyond that, advancing the developer's temperature to 90°, just a few degrees below the maximum considered safe for the emulsion. Finally he printed on extra-contrasty grade 6 paper, which made the contrasts as strong as those in the most vivid newspaper picture.

deFRANCIS: *Counterpoint*, 1970

Shadows to Startle the Eye

RENÉ BURRI: *Shadow of a Tree,* 1963

Like a thick black-velvet carpet that divides into narrow strips radiating out to cover the desert, the shadow of a tree links foreground to background in this picture, which was shot near the city of Rawalpindi in West Pakistan. Rohtas Fort, a 40-foot-thick, three-mile-long wall that was built in the 16th Century, stretches across the far horizon in a geometric frieze.

Every photographer who has ever glanced at a manual knows that he must watch out for shadows; they obtrude into pictures, obscure subjects, distract viewers from the point of the picture. Far from being awkward mistakes that stamp the pictures as the work of amateurs, the shadows in the photographs on these pages command attention—and make the pictures successful. René Burri's tree shadow (opposite), its sparse branches spreading out over a backdrop of dry, rocky terrain, forms a pattern that seems to have a palpable texture of its own. Ken Josephson's shadow image of himself snapping his infant son makes the baby appear to be floating in a state of suspension against a vertical wall. Josephson decided to present himself, the photographer, as a presence visible along with his subject. He liked the result so well that he used it on his holiday greeting cards for the year.

His father's shadow looms above and below two-month-old Matthew Josephson, lying asleep on the grass. The picture was shot on a bright, sunshiny day and overexposed slightly to make sure that the image of the baby would emerge clearly from its dark surroundings.

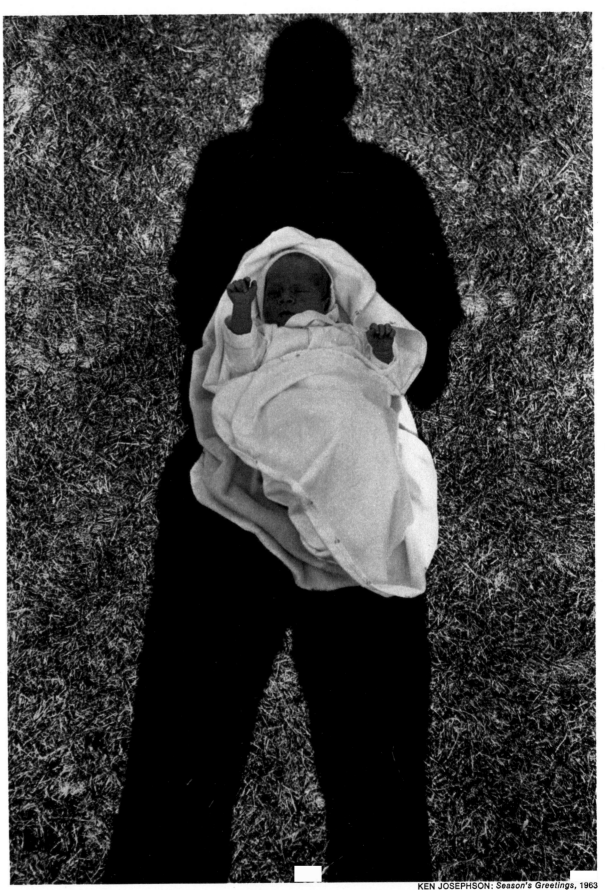

KEN JOSEPHSON: *Season's Greetings,* 1963

Drama from the Misused Film

KAMI: *Self-Portrait,* 1969

Using the wrong film the wrong way sometimes produces the right results, as these arresting portraits illustrate. All were made with slow film that was severely underexposed and then overdeveloped. Such treatment causes a contrasty image: many of the slow emulsion's crystals are too little affected by light to be developed, leaving blank areas; those that are affected by light are completely converted to metallic silver by prolonged development, creating very dense exposed areas. The higher contrast lessens tonal gradations and can, as in these pictures, create striking, almost theatrical lights and darks for a portrait.

Conversely, if a fast film is overexposed and underdeveloped, the contrasts are flattened. This combination, too, may give just the right result if a photographer has shot a subject—for instance, a beach house in bright sun—that has very bright highlights and dark shadows. When overexposed during printing or enlarging, the entire image may take on a greenish-black tone, effective, for instance, in giving a rural landscape an evocative tint reminiscent of old-time photographs.

When Richard Kam, who signs his work with the diminutive Kami, took his own picture, he exposed for the fast ASA 400 film he thought he had. It was actually a slow ASA 64 film, so he overdeveloped it in a highly concentrated solution—exaggerating contrast to create a striking old-fashioned flavor for his self-portrait.

KAMI: *Series Portrait,* 1969

Kam purposely used the same technique and film to enhance contrast for dramatic effect in these portraits of a San Francisco girl. The film is a special copying type, formulated to produce readable reproductions of book and newspaper pages, and has very fine grain. This characteristic prevented the graininess that often results from prolonged development.

Making a Point by Chopping Off Heads

ANTHONY SZCZYGIELSKI: *Varsity Club, Palmyra, New York*, 1970

One of the first things a photographer learns is not to take pictures that chop off people's heads. Decapitation is easy to do in close-ups made with some cameras that have a viewfinder lens separate from the taking lens. Unless the two lenses are interconnected, the photographer sees a slightly different view of the subject from the view that will go through the lens to the film. And even with cameras that display on their viewing screens exactly what the film will record, part of a head may inadvertently be left out if a photographer is shooting on the run and fails to frame his composition on the screen. The loss, particularly of the eyes, may rob the picture of its most expressive elements—but, by directing attention to other elements, a partial image of the subject may say a great deal more than a complete view possibly could.

This group shot was taken with a 24mm wide-angle lens to get everybody in the frame—but without their heads. The picture was meant to emphasize the social nature of students, and eliminating heads concentrates the essence of the idea, revealing the young people's emotional interrelationship through the linkage of their hands and the closeness of their bodies.

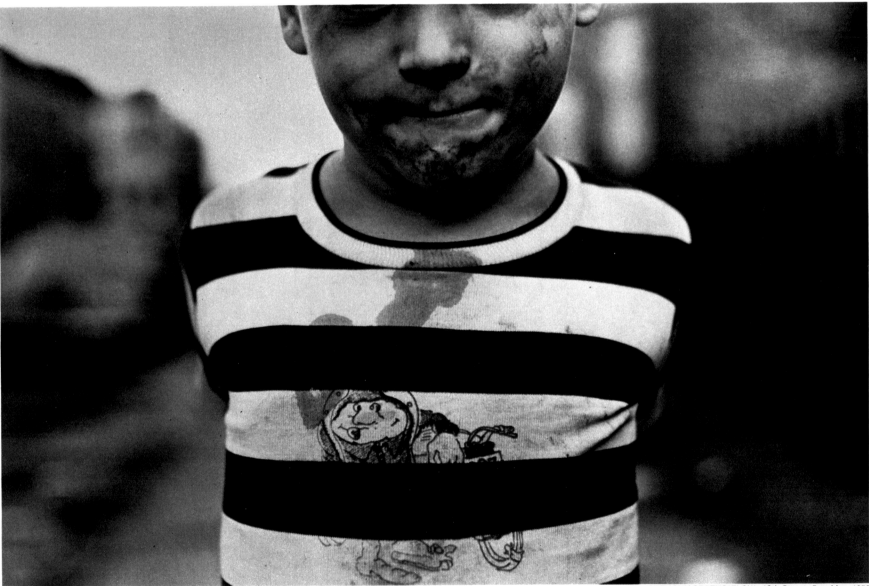

ANTHONY SZCZYGIELSKI: *12th Street, Brooklyn, 1970*

This picture is part of a study Anthony Szczygielski made of neighborhood youngsters, of whom he says, "Dirt and ice cream are a quality of childhood, or at least of this group of kids—they're rambunctious and proud of being dirty." He composed the picture deliberately to crop off the top of the boy's head, thus underlining the cocky bravado of the facial expression and the pulled-back shoulders beneath the ice-cream-streaked T-shirt.

The Power of Distorted Perspective

HARVEY DUZE: *Variation,* 1970

The strange twists in perspective a camera can give—sometimes comic, sometimes menacing—are distortions that also occur ordinarily in human vision. But when the eye sees them, the brain ignores them.

If the eye registers a nearby midget identical in size to a far-off giant, the incongruity is dismissed. When the effect is presented in a photograph, however, it seems ludicrous. To the eye the vertical lines of a tall building appear to converge toward the top. But if a photograph shows the sides of a building as anything but parallel *(right),* the brain seeks special meaning in a seemingly false image.

When distortion of perspective does not correspond to natural perception, it seems even more ridiculous. For example, though the normal horizontal angle of vision is almost 180°, the same wide viewing angle that a 7.5mm fisheye lens takes in, the image produced by such a lens appears distorted because it is unfamiliar; the brain is only dimly conscious of peripheral areas. When a fisheye view is reproduced on the flat plane of a photograph *(opposite),* it yields distortion that in human vision the brain ignores: horizontal lines bend in at the edges of the pictures.

◄ *A 12mm fisheye lens, which gives an angle of view of 150°, bends the lines of an A-frame cabin shot through the windshield of a car about 20 feet away. Size distortion is also noticeable in the exaggeratedly large image of the dashboard handle in the center foreground.*

A homely object of ridicule—an old privy—is made to appear ominous by altering perspective so the top of the structure seems larger than the bottom. The distorted perspective was achieved with a view camera, whose adjustable back tilted the film holder at an unusual angle.

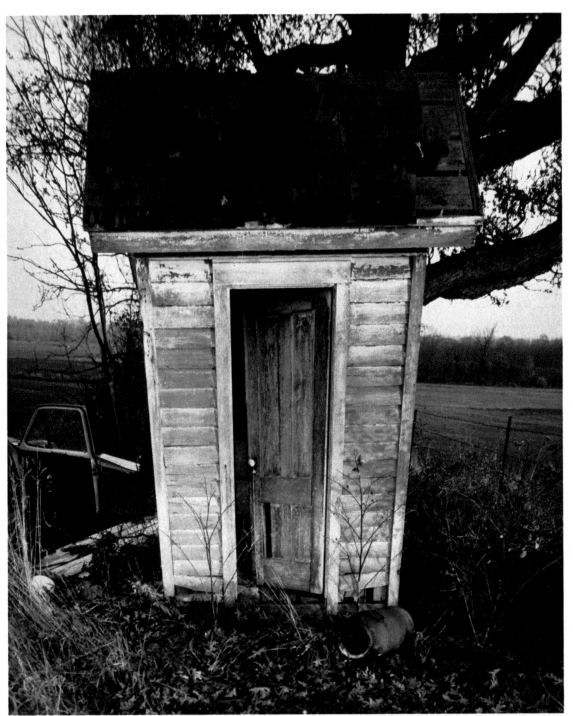

JOHN GRAHAM LAMB: *Threatening Outhouse,* 1970

Tampering with Lenses to Break Up the Light

MARCIA KEEGAN: *Tunnel*, 1970

Dirt or scratches on a lens ordinarily ruin pictures but they can make bright light do strange and often useful tricks. When the effect is sought deliberately, the lens is not touched, of course; the light manipulation is achieved by using a filter as the front element in the camera's optical system.

The result depends on how the lens is "dirtied." A substance like water or grease—petroleum jelly, for instance —adds an extra refracting surface to bend light rays, smearing the focus created by the lens itself *(opposite).*

Solid specks of dirt and scratches cause an optically different kind of interference called diffraction. The edges of such an obstruction partially block the front of a light wave, in effect twisting the wave into a new direction. This spreading, or diffusion, of light waves can create an overall softness. Soft-focus lens attachments—clear filters incised with various line patterns— serve the same purpose. And in dim light some of these attachments transform whatever sources of bright light are present into stars *(above).*

Stalled in traffic in a dim tunnel, Marcia Keegan decided to emphasize the glare of the tunnel and vehicle lights with diffraction effects. She put a cross-screen filter—clear glass with fine vertical and horizontal engraved lines—over a 35mm wide-angle lens and took the photograph above, exposing at f/4 for 1/60 second. The four-pointed flares that make light sources look like stars result from the interaction between the light waves and the filter's lines.

MARCIA KEEGAN: *Circus*, 1967

To get this shot of a Ringling Bros. and Barnum & Bailey performance in full swing, the outer rim of a clear glass filter was coated with petroleum jelly, then placed over the regular 50mm lens on a 35mm camera. When the light hit the grease coating, it blurred the periphery of the picture, in contrast with the sharp center focus.

For Mystery, Focus on the Wrong Thing

BENNO FRIEDMAN: *Untitled,* 1969

Because long lenses have restricted depth of field, Benno Friedman used one, a 200mm, on his Nikkormat camera to get the shallow focus that emphasizes the tree trunk while blurring the man's figure. Actually, the tree, which was 15 or 20 feet away from Friedman, was only about 15 feet in front of the man, whose back is to it.

Obviously, the chief aim of the photographer is to produce a clear image of the main element in his picture. He is taught to adjust his camera's depth of field to get that element in focus, even at the expense of blurring its surroundings. And he learns to avoid shooting through any foreground obstruction that might confuse its outlines. Yet he may violate these rules with profit if his purpose is ambiguity; one way to endow a subject with mystery is to make it prominent but somehow secondary.

The young man in the photograph opposite is the true subject of the picture, but his image has been thrown out of focus, and contrasts with the slender tree trunk in the left foreground that is depicted in relatively clear detail. The car is the main element in the picture at right, but its lines are half-submerged in the texture of the curtain through which the camera was aimed.

The great depth of field of a wide-angle 28mm lens solved the problem of balancing the objects in this composition. The lens got sharp detail in the window curtain in the foreground, making this subordinate element seem almost as important as the car in the street, which stands out because it too is in focus.

BENNO FRIEDMAN: *Untitled,* 1969

193

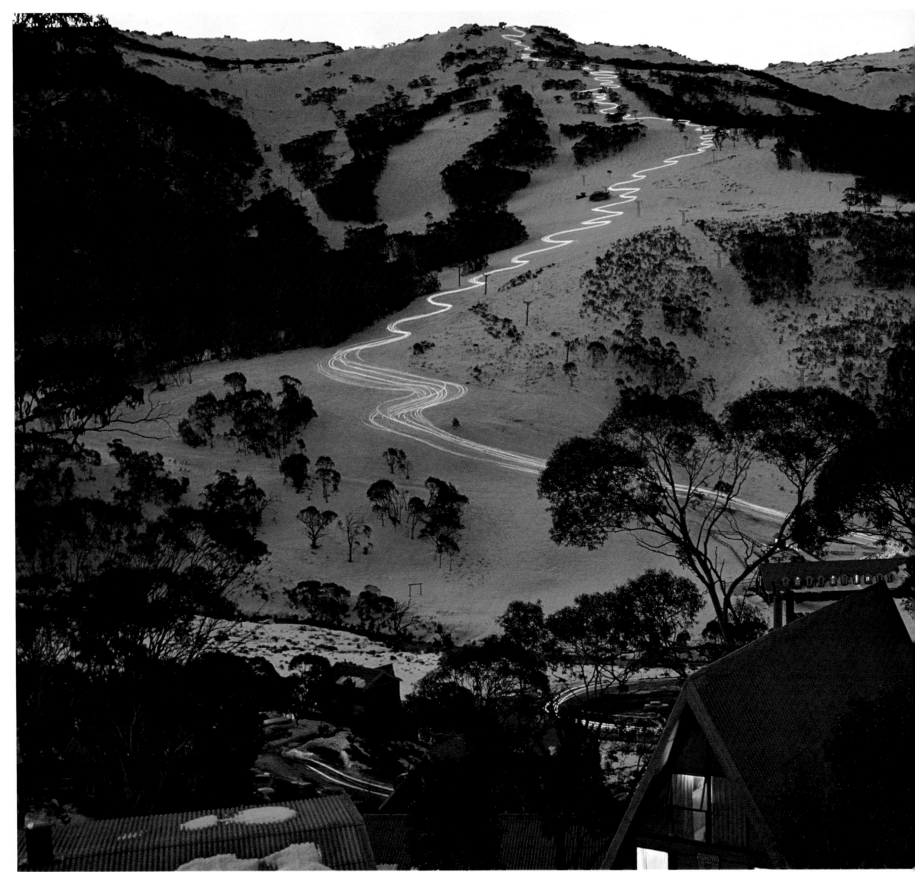

DAVID MOORE: *Torchlight Procession ot Skiers, Australia,* 1966

194

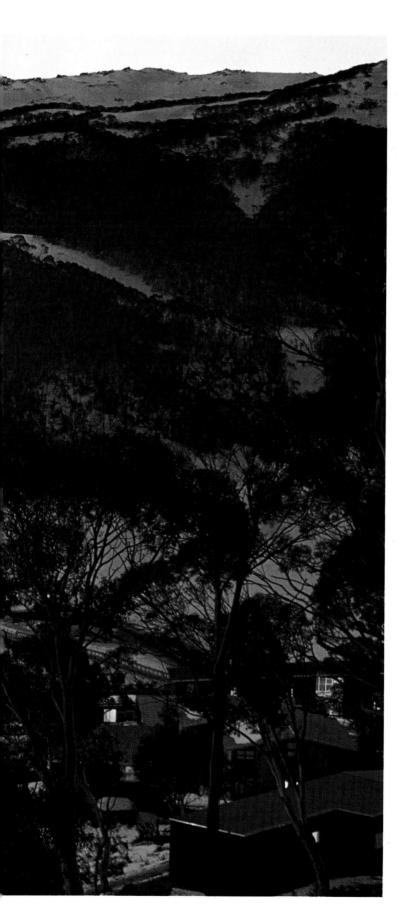

Mellow Tints from Reciprocity Failure

PETER DeLORY: *Summer,* 1970

The warm purple tint over the snow (left) and the two-toned sky in the picture above were produced by reciprocity failure. Both pictures were shot in the dim light of dusk and given lengthy exposures; David Moore exposed for the

full five minutes it took the skiers to run the trail (the zigzag thread of light that bisects his picture). To avoid overexposure, he set his aperture at its smallest opening, f/22, thus reducing the amount of light admitted.

The "law of reciprocity" states that a long exposure in very dim light should give exactly the same result as a short exposure in very bright light. (In technical terms, the effects of light intensity and exposure time are reciprocal; an increase in one factor precisely counterbalances a decrease in the other.) That's the law. Film emulsions obey it —most of the time. But the law breaks down if film is exposed for more than five seconds in an extremely dim light, or for less than 1/1000 of a second in a very strong light; then the phenomenon known as "reciprocity failure" occurs.

Its cause is not entirely understood; most experts think it results when light is insufficiently intense to trigger the silver bromide crystals in film into forming a latent image. Reciprocity failure slows the speed of the film, which gives an underexposed, darkened black-and-white image. Something more happens with color films. Because they contain three separate emulsion layers, each of which may be affected differently, the varied speed losses change color balance. The result is color shifts, like those that give a pleasing cast to the two pictures shown on these pages.

Sun Shots to Turn Day into Night

It takes some daring to flout the don't-shoot-into-the-sun convention, for no photographer can be certain how such a shot will come out. The sun's light is so bright that it can easily swamp the film, obliterating most of the image through overexposure. If the photographer follows the usual prescription for backlighted scenes and exposes for the darker areas to register their detail, overexposure is almost certain to result. But if he reverses the procedure and exposes for the brightest areas, striking moonlight effects can be obtained in daytime *(right)*.

It is easiest to make day-for-night shots when the sun is brilliantly strong and low in the sky; then it creates conditions more easily transformed into an illusion of moonlight: it generates areas of shadow that provide contrast, and it also spreads strong reflections over open expanses, especially those that include snow or—as at right—water. The effect depends on what could be termed extreme underexposure, especially if the sun's image is to be included in the picture. (Even so, it is likely to appear as the white glare seen at the top of this photograph.) If the combination of highest shutter speed with smallest aperture provides insufficient underexposure to get the night-scene effect, a filter will reduce still further the amount of light reaching the film. A deep-red filter is very effective, for it darkens shadows, emphasizes contrasts and almost blackens the sky.

To get spectral light effects in the middle of the day, Walter Iooss Jr. reduced the amount of light that entered his 35mm camera by shooting at an extremely fast speed (1/1000 second) and stopping down his aperture to a tiny f/16. For breadth of view and depth of field, he used a 28mm lens. Such wide-angle lenses are often used for landscapes because they can keep in focus areas as deep as that extending from the reeds in the foreground to the clouds in the background. At the same time wide-angle lenses permit the inclusion of an expanse as broad as that of the center plane, where land, water and more land stretch across the horizon.

WALTER IOOSS JR.: *Hawaii*, 1966

Sacrificing Detail to Create a Mood

BILL BINZEN: *End of the Day—Trinidad,* 1967

*Even with exposure of two seconds at f/2.8, the
backlighted little girl in the foreground of
this dusk scene was underexposed. Bill Binzen
also omitted the pale blue or pale green filter
sometimes used to help tone down the
excessive redness of twilight. The brilliant
orange of his background is the actual color he
remembers seeing in the sky and water.*

Both the pictures shown here were made with backlighting so strong that the figures become silhouettes almost entirely devoid of any detail. But each achieves its particular effect through a different technique.

Backlighting alone can eliminate detail, as at left, if the usual exposure recommendations are ignored. Exposing for the brightest parts of a scene instead of the dimmest reduces the most prominent elements to silhouettes and greatly simplifies the ideas they express—in this case the girl's posture and her placement in the scene convey a single impression, that of a quiet thoughtfulness.

Quite another feeling is suggested if the picture is not only silhouetted by backlighting but also thrown out of focus and overexposed *(right).* Detail is again eliminated, but now outlines are also distorted, partly because overexposure tends to spread the effect of bright light. This spilling over of light may wash out narrow dark areas such as the arms of this dancer, which are so thinned that the figure becomes an exuberant, unearthly wraith.

To catch the gaiety of a young woman frolicking on a Cape Cod beach on a summer day, Whitney L. Lane "played around with the focus until I got a blurry, elongated silhouette," then shot at 1/125 and f/4. This overexposure further blurred the image and made the girl seem as ephemeral as a water sprite come to life.

WHITNEY L. LANE: *Sea Nymph,* 1970

An Inferior Lens for Superior Effects

One reason for the high price of a good camera lens is the need for several separate elements, each shaped to work with the others in creating a sharp image. But a sharp image, every line and color in its proper place, would have dissipated the charm of the picture at right, which was made with a simple lens similar to a magnifying glass and prone to the defects so expensively removed from a fine camera lens.

A simple lens made of a single piece of convex glass causes blur in a number of ways. For one thing, it cannot get the edges of the image into sharp focus (unless the aperture used is extremely small); to correct that error, at least one other, differently shaped lens element must be added. For another, the single lens makes overlapping images of each of the colors in the spectrum. It bends each color to a different degree, thus splitting a ray of light into its component colors and bringing each of these separate components to a focus at a different point on the film. Correcting this "chromatic aberration" requires another lens element to cancel the color effects of the first; it must be made of a different kind of glass and shaped to bend light in a compensating direction. Because it lacks such corrections, the simple lens seldom produces a faithful reproduction of a subject—but it can transcend direct reproduction to create scenes of unusual beauty.

"This was a different approach to shooting fall—an attempt to capture pattern, line and design in an abstract view of fall foliage," says Henry A. Shull of his close-up of a sprig of maple, which he found beginning to turn color on an overcast October day in Vermont. He photographed it from a distance of two or three feet, using a Nikon set at f/2 and 1/500—but with the standard lens replaced by a piece of convex optical glass. This simple lens blends colors together to create surprising shades in the developed print.

HENRY A. SHULL: *Autumn Leaves*, 1970

Indoor Film to Create a New View of the Outdoor World

STEPHEN GREEN-ARMYTAGE: *Two Boys Fishing*, 1970

If a photographer wants a blue tone in his outdoor scenes he can use indoor color film, which is very sensitive to blue light. When the film is used indoors this weighting counterbalances artificial light's lack of blue and over- abundance of red, making the result look natural. Outdoors, where light colors often tend toward the blue, it can give a pleasantly monochromatic effect. (Conversely, outdoor film used indoors gives yellowish-red results.) ☐

When indoor film is used to take a picture in daylight, the result is the blue cast that gives this picture its distinctive quality. Photographer Stephen Green-Armytage could have "corrected" his color to achieve naturalistic lighting by using a yellow filter, but he preferred the monochromatic tints because he felt they would simplify the content of his picture.

Bibliography

Adams, Ansel, *Natural-Light Photography.* Morgan & Morgan, 1952.

*Birnbaum, Hugh, and Don Sutherland, *Photo Guide for Travelers.* Rivoli Press, 1970.

Croy, O. R., *Creative Photography.* Focal Press, 1965.

*Department of the Navy "Photographic Bulletin —Tips for Cold Weather Photography." COMNAVSUPPFOR.

Evans, Ralph M., *Eye, Film and Camera in Color Photography.* Wiley, 1969.

Eastman Kodak:
Adventures in Existing-Light Photography, Photo Information Book AC-44. Eastman Kodak, 1969.

Color Photography Outdoors, Color Data Book E-75. Eastman Kodak, 1969.

Kodak Black-and-White Films in Rolls, Photo Information Book AF-13. Eastman Kodak, 1967.

Kodak Color Films, Color Data Book E-77. Eastman Kodak, 1968.

Notes on Tropical Photography, Service Pamphlet C-24. Eastman Kodak, 1958.

Photography under Arctic Conditions, Pamphlet C-9. Eastman Kodak, 1967.

Prevention and Removal of Fungus on Processed Films, Service Pamphlet AE-22. Eastman Kodak, 1966.

Focal Press Ltd., *Focal Encyclopedia of Photography.* McGraw-Hill, 1969.

Fritsche, Kurt, *Faults in Photography: Causes and Correctives.* Focal Press, 1968.

*Hertzberg, Robert E., *Photo Darkroom Guide.* Amphoto, 1967.

*Jonas, Paul, *Manual of Darkroom Procedures and Techniques.* Amphoto, 1967.

Mees, C. E. Kenneth, *From Dry Plates to Ektachrome Film.* Ziff-Davis, 1961.

Mueller, Conrad G., and Mae Rudolph and the Editors of TIME-LIFE Books, *Light and Vision.* TIME-LIFE Books, 1969.

Pittaro, Ernest M., *Photo-Lab-Index.* Morgan & Morgan, 1970.

Smith, Edwin, *All the Photo Tricks.* Focal Press, 1959.

Spencer, D. A., *Color Photography in Practice.* Focal Press, 1966.

Periodicals

Aperture, Aperture Inc., New York City

British Journal of Photography, Henry Greenwood and Co., London

Camera, C. J. Bucher Ltd., Lucerne, Switzerland

Camera 35, U.S. Camera Publishing Co., New York City

Creative Camera, International Federation of Amateur Photographers, London

Infinity, American Society of Magazine Photographers, New York City

Modern Photography, The Billboard Publishing Co., New York City

Popular Photography, Ziff-Davis Publishing Co., New York City

Travel & Camera, U.S. Camera Publishing Corp., New York City

U.S. Camera World Annual, U.S. Camera Publishing Corp., New York City

*Available only in paperback.

Acknowledgments

For the help given in the preparation of this book, the editors would like to express their gratitude to Walter Clark, Rochester, New York; George A. Doumani, Science Policy Research Divison, Library of Congress, Washington, D.C.; Werner A. Fallet, Assistant Sales Manager, Zeiss-Ikon-Voigtlander of America, Inc., New York City; Martin Forscher, Professional Camera Repair Service Inc., New York City; Alfred Geller, Royaltone Inc., New York City; William Harmon, Nikon Inc., Garden City, N.Y.; Rudolf Kingslake, Retired Director of Optical Design, Eastman Kodak Co., Rochester, N.Y.; Phillip Leonian, New York City; Robert E. Mayer, Manager, Photographic Services, Bell & Howell Photo Sales Co., Chicago, Illinois; from the Rochester Institute of Technology, Rochester, N.Y.: Lothar K. Engelmann, Dean of College of Graphic Arts and Photography, William S. Shoemaker, Director of School of Photographic Arts and Sciences, John F. Carson, Staff Chairman, Photographic Science and Instrumentation, Edwin M. Wilson, Staff Chairman, Professional Photography, Tom Muir Wilson, Staff Chairman, Photographic Illustration, and the faculty and staff of the School of Photographic Arts and Sciences; Cleveland C. Soper, Research Associate, Eastman Kodak Co., Rochester, N.Y.; Mike Sutkowski, Office of Public Relations, Singer Diversified Worldwide, New York City.

Picture Credits Credits from left to right are separated by semicolons, from top to bottom by dashes.

Index *Numerals in italics indicate a photograph, painting or drawing of the subject mentioned.*

Aberrations: and resolution of lens, 106; for special effects, *200-201*
Adams, Ansel, 158
Agitation in processing, effect of insufficient, *123*
Air bubbles on film in developer, symptoms of, *122*
Angle of camera: and elimination of distracting backgrounds, 50, *51;* and elimination of flare, *56-57;* and elimination of reflections, *53;* and stop-action photography, 130, 143, 152
Armstrong-Jones, Antony, 95
Auto-collimator, 112, *113*

Backgrounds: elimination of distracting, 46-47, *50-51;* error of unnoticed, 92-93; retention of, in portrait, 60-61
Backlighting, *198-199*
Baker, Irving, *161*
Barrel distortion, 62; revealed by test chart, 106, *107*
Barstow, Jim, photograph by, *166*
Barton, Hugh, 162; photograph by, *163*
Bavagnoli, Carlo: photographs by, *86, 87;* and reversal of lens for photomacrography, 86
Bicycle-pump shutter release, 70, 72
Binzen, Bill, 198; photograph by, *198*
Blank frames, significance of, 114
Blank white areas on print, *120-121;* significance of, 114, 120-121
Blur: and aberrations, 106, *200-201;* and depth of field, *48-49*, 50, *51*, *54-55*, *192;* and greased filter, 190, *191;* and photography of motion, *127, 129, 131-132, 146, 147, 148-149, 170-171*
Burri, René, 183; photograph by, *182*

Camera(s): bodies, extra, 25; housing, nitrogen-filled, *76;* housing, waterproof, *18*, 20-21, 151; malfunctions of, 102-103, *114-124;* motorized, 76-81, 131, 133, 136, 151; repairs of, in the field, 24-25; slit, 134, 140, 146; tests for, *104-113*
Camera and equipment care: in cold environments, *19*, 22-24, 36, 40; in dry environments, 21-22; in dusty environments, *18*, 21-22, 26, 32; in hot environments, 13-14, *19*, 96; in humid environments, 15, 17, *19;* in wet environments, *18*, 20-21, 31, 35
Chemicals, effect of stale, 122, 123
Circo-Mirrotach, *45, 68*
Cold environments: effects of, on exposure meters, 23; effects of, on film, 22-24; effects of, on lenses, 22; effects of, on shutters, 22, 36; effects of snow-covered terrain on exposure, 23; freezing of skin to equipment, 22, 23, 40; photographs taken in, *cover, 36-37, 38-39, 40-41, 42;* protection of equipment in, *19*, 22-24, 38, 40
Collodion emulsion, 26

Color shift, and reciprocity failure, *194-195;* and improper use of color film, *202*
Condenser enlarger, 58
Contact sheet, for diagnosis of equipment malfunction, *114-124*
Contrast, high, 180; intentional, *163, 180-181, 184-185*
Cooke, Jerry, and radio-controlled cameras, 79
Crane, Ralph, *13*, 14
Cropping, for special effects, *186-187*
Crowds, photographing over the heads of, *66-67, 97*

Darkroom, emergency, 24-25
Darkroom errors, *122-123*, 124
Defects appearing on contact sheet: blank frames, 114; blank white areas, 114, *120-121, 122-123;* dark splotches, 122; dark streaks, *123;* diffused images, *117;* image cutoff, 114, *116, 118-119;* "lightning" stroke, *124;* multiple exposures, 114, *115;* vignetting, 114, *116*
deFrancis, Peter, 180; photograph by, *180-181*
DeLory, Peter, photograph by, *194*
Depth of field: and diffusion of backgrounds, 47, *50-51;* and diffusion of foregrounds, *48-49;* and photographing reflections, *54-55*, 177; and portraits preserving background detail, *60-61;* and selection of main picture elements, *192-193*
Developers, high-contrast, 180
Development, for high-contrast, 180, 184
Diaphragm: malfunction of, 108; test for, 108, 109
Diffraction, for special effects, *190*
Diffused images, significance of, 117
Diffusion enlarger, 58, 59
Distance, and stop-action photography, 130
Distortions: barrel, *62*, 106, *107;* intentional, 177
Dominis, John, 31, 32; photographs by, *31, 32;* and unnoticed detail, 93
Double-pole double-throw momentary contact switch, 72, 73
Doumani, George A., 39; photographs by, *38-39*
Drage, Derek, 168
Drake, James, 139, 152; photographs by, *138-139, 152*
Dressen, Chuck, 98
Dry environments, equipment problems in, 21-22
Dust on negatives, symptoms of, 122
Dusty environments: effects of, on camera mechanism, 21; effects of, on film, 21; effects of, on lenses, 21; photographs taken in, *cover, 28-29, 32;* protection of equipment in, *19*, 21-22, 26, 32
Dutton, Allen, photograph by, *cover*
Duze, Harvey, photograph by, *188*

Early, Dennis, 170; photograph by, *170*
Eastman Kodak Co., 158

Education in photography, 158-172; Rochester Institute of Technology, *157-172*
Eisenstaedt, Alfred, 94; and photographing over crowds, 97
Electronic flash. *See* Strobe lights, electronic
Electrostatic discharge, film exposed by, 22, 24, 96, *124*
Emulsion(s), effect of physical environment on collodion, 26
Enlargers, condenser vs. diffusion, 58, 59
Eppridge, Bill, photographs by, *157-161*
Equipment care: in cold environments, *19*, 22-24, 36, 40; in dry environments, 21-22; in dusty environments, *18*, 21-22, 26, 32; in hot environments, 13-14, *19*, 96; in humid environments, 15, 17, *19;* in wet environments, *18*, 20-21, 31, 35
Equipment for special problems: bicycle-pump shutter release, 70, 72; motor-driven tripod head, 74, 75, 76; nitrogen-filled camera housing, 76, 77; remote control for cameras and strobe lights, 78, 79-80; sequential switch for strobe lights, *74;* switch for combination time-strobe exposures, 72, *73;* timers for motorized cameras, 76, 77, 78
Equipment for sports photography, 132-133; helicopter, 150; motorized camera, 133, 136, 151; slit camera, 134, 140, 146; strobe lights, 129, 144
Equipment for testing cameras: at home, *104-111;* professional, *112-113*
Errors, profiting from, 92-98
Exposure(s): affected by snow-covered terrain, 23; calculation in Antarctic conditions, 39; for day-into-night effect, *196-197;* in desert, 26; very long, 90, *194-195*
Exposure meters: in cold environments, 23; effects of water on, 20, 32; selenium vs. cadmium sulfide cells, *19*, 23
Exposures, multiple, *88-89, 101, 115;* intentional, *88-89*, 176-177, *115;* significance of, 114, 115; using masks for, *88-89*
Extension rings, for photomacrography, 86, *87*

Film: effects of cold on, 23-24, 96; effects of dust on, 21; effects of fungus on, 15; effects of heat and humidity on, 14-17, 96; effects of moth and mildew repellents on, 17; effects of water on, 20; high-contrast, 180, 184, 185; high-resolution, for testing lenses, 106; incorrectly loaded into camera, 94-95; incorrectly loaded into developing tank, 122; indoor vs. outdoor color, 202; reciprocity failure of, 195; slow film and long exposures, 90
Film-advance mechanism: manipulation of, for intentional

double exposures, 176-177; symptoms of malfunction of, 114, *115*
Filters: cross-screen, 190; to enhance contrast, 90; fog-illusion, 82; as lens protectors, 21, 28, 35; polarizing, 47, 52-53; red and yellow, 47; skylight (ultraviolet), 23; split, 47, 82; and vignetting, 116
Fixer, stale, effect of, *123*
Flare: prevention of, *56-57;* use of, *190*
Focusing system, test of, 112, *113*
Fog, illusion of, 82, *83*
Foregrounds, diffusing of distracting, *48-49*
Freezing motion. *See* Stop-motion photography
Freni, Al, 147; photograph by, *147*
Friedman, Benno, 192; photographs by, *192, 193*
Fungus: effects of, on film, 14; effects of, on lens, 14; protection against, 15, 17, 30

Gaffer tape, *19*, 25
Glatzel, Erhard, 62
Gleason, Judie, 172; photograph by, *172*
Gonzales, Pancho, 93
Goodman, Robert B., 28; photographs by, *28-29*
Goro, Fritz, and camera malfunction, 102
Graininess, 176, 185; causes of, 178; intentional, *178-179*
Green-Armytage, Stephen, 202
Groskinsky, Henry, 14; and exposure of hot lamps to precipitation, 94

Haling, George, demonstration of elimination of distracting background, *50-51*
Harrod, Denny, 161
Haskell, Jonathan, photographs by, *165*
Hattersley, Ralph, 162
Hayes, Keith J., 97
Hayes, Mrs. Keith J., *96*, 97
Hockman, Mark, *169*
Hofer, Evelyn, and long exposures, 90; photographs by, *58-59, 91*
Hogan, Ben, 94
Hologon (lens), 15mm, 62, 63
Hot environments: effects of, on cameras, 12-13, 14; effects of, on film, 14-15, 17, 96; photographs taken in, *cover, 27, 28-29, 30, 31;* protection of equipment in, 13-15, 17, *19*
Huljack, Greg, photograph by, *165*
Humid environments: and heat, effects of, on film, 14-17; photographs taken in, *30, 31;* protection of film in, 15, 17, *19*
Hunt, Keith, photograph by, *165*

Ice, on cameras and lenses, 22-23
Image cutoff, *118-119;* intentional, *186*, 187; significance of, 118-119. *See also* Vignetting
Image intensifier tube, 64

looss, Walter, Jr., 133, 134, 196; photographs by, 124, 134-135, 196-197

Jacobson, Gerald: photographs by, 84-85, 101; and of shadows, 84
Jensen, Paul, demonstration of diffusion of distracting foreground, 48-49
Joel, Yale, 71; and bicycle-pump shutter release, 70, 72; and motor-driven tripod head, 74, 75, 76; photographs by, 71, 75
Johansson, Ingemar, 136-137
Johnson, Lyndon B., 95
Josephson, Ken, 183

Kami (Richard Kam), 184, 185; photographs by, 184-185
Kauffman, Mark, 92; and the "easy" subject, 97-98; and equipment in the desert, 96; and hole in shutter, 95; and the ignored picture, 98; and incorrectly loaded film, 94-95; and incorrectly wired strobe lights, 93-94; and photographing in crowds, 97; photographs by, 96-97, 98; and shutter noise, 94; tales of, 92-98; and tripod substitute, 95; and uninformed subject, 97; and unnoticed background, 92-93
Keegan, Marcia, photographs by, 190, 191
Kellerhouse, Karen, photograph by, 164
Keshen, Cary, 161
Kidd, Billy, 146
Kirman, Charles, 171; photograph by, 171
Kober, Fritz, 62
Krukowski, Dennis, photograph by, 166

Lamb, John Graham, photograph by, 189
Lane, Whitney L., 199; photograph by, 199
Lansbury, Angela, 92
Lean, David, 96
Leifer, Neil: photographs by, 146, 150; and sports photography, 132, 134, 146, 150
Lens(es): aberrations of, 106, 200; Circo-Mirrotach attachment, 68; cleaning of, 117; effects of dirt on, 21, 117, 190; effects of fungus on, 14; effects of heat on, 12-13; effects of high pressure on, 78; fisheye, 188; and flare, 56, 190; Hologon, 15mm, 62-63; ice on, 23; inferior, for special effects, 200; long focal length, 47, 48, 50, 139, 140, 152, 192; manipulated, 190-191; "periscope," 47, 68; resolution test for, 104-105; reversal of, for photomacrography, 86, 87; split-field, 46, 60-61; and vignetting, 114, 116; wide-angle, 47, 149, 152, 177, 193, 196; zoom, 132, 154. See also Equipment care
Lens shade, 18; and vignetting, 116
Leonian, Phillip, photograph by, 127
LIFE Photo Lab: equipment inventory of, 80; special equipment of, 72-81
Light bulbs, exposure of, to precipitation, 94
Light leak, symptoms of, 96, 114, 120-121
"Lightning" stroke in print, 22, 24, 96, 124
Low-light-level camera system, 47, 64, 65; applications of, 64

McCombe, Leonard, 35; photograph by, 34-35
McLain, Denny, 153
McQuade, John, photograph by, 164
Margaret, Princess, 95
Masks, for multiple exposures, 88, 89
Mercouri, Melina, 97
Mildew. See Fungus
Miller, Mike, 113
Mirrors: photographs of objects in, 54-55; in right-angle lens attachment, 68
Mistakes, profiting from, 92-98
Mold. See Fungus
Mood of picture: and elimination of detail, 58-59, 178, 198-199; and optical system of enlarger, 58-59
Moore, Charles, 26; photograph by, 27
Moore, David, 195; photograph by, 194-195
Morse, Gary, 160
Morse, Ralph: and direct-wire remote control, 80, 81; and lenses exposed to high pressures, 78; and multiple exposures using masks, 88-89; photographs by, 81, 89; and timers to control cameras, 77, 78
Motion, photography of, 73, 75, 127, 128-133, 134-154, 170-171; by blurring, 127, 129, 131-132, 170-171; and camera angle, 130; and panning, 130-131; and peak action, 129-130; in sequences, 129, 131, 136; with slit camera, 134, 140, 146; special equipment for, 72, 73, 74, 75, 76; and sports, 132-133; 134-154
Motion analyzer, 113
Motor-driven tripod head, 74, 75, 76
Motorized cameras, 76, 77-81, 94, 99, 106, 111, 133, 136, 140, 146, 151; and electrostatic discharges, 124; and sequences of photographs, 131, 136
Multiple exposures. See Exposures, multiple

National Geographic, The, magazine, 103
Neckstraps: effect of perspiration on, 20; metal, 20
Nitrogen-filled camera housing, 76
Nkrumah, Kwame, 93-94
Nunley, Robert R., 40; photograph by, 40-41

Olson, John, 36; photograph by, 36-37
Osborne, Walter D., 154; photograph by, 154
O'Toole, Peter, 96

Panning, 127, 130-131, 148; and motor-driven tripod head, 74, 75, 76, 147, 148-149
Patterson, Floyd, 136-137
Peak action, 129-130, 142
Pelham, Lynn, photograph by, 142
People, elimination of, when obstructing subject, 90, 91
Perspective, distortion of, 177, 188-189
Perspiration, effect of, on equipment, 20
Phosphorescent tape, for testing shutter synchronization, 110, 111
Photography, education in, 158-172; Rochester Institute of Technology, 157-172
Photomacrography, with reversed lens, 86, 87
Polarized light, from reflections, 52
Polarizing filter, to eliminate reflections, 47, 52-53
Prefocusing, 133, 147
Pressure plate: and excessive film tension, 114; and image sharpness, 104
Processing errors, 122-123

Races, radio-controlled cameras to photograph, 79
Range finder, and image sharpness, 104
Raymond, Lilo, 176; photograph by, 176-177
Reciprocity failure, 195; for special effects, 194-195
Reflections: elimination of, 52-53; photographing objects and their reflections, 54-55, 168, 169, 177
Relays, for remote control of motorized cameras, 80
Remote control: direct-wire, for cameras, 79, 80; radio, for cameras, 78, 79, 80; radio, for strobe lights, 78
Rentmeester, Co, 20, 32; and camera malfunction, 102; photograph by, 33
Repairs, camera, emergency, 24-25
Resolving power, of lenses, 104-105
Rochester Institute of Technology: Biomedical Photography, 159; facilities of, 160-161; Photographic Science and Instrumentation, 159; School of Photographic Arts and Sciences, 157-172; School of Printing, 160
Rocket launchings, special equipment to photograph, 76, 77
Rougier, Michael, 30; photograph by, 30
Rules, creative breaking of, 175-202

Salt water: effects of, on equipment, 20; emergency treatment for immersion of camera in, 20. See also Wet environments
Sandwiching, 177
Sapp, Theron, 134-135
Scheller, Donald, 168; photograph by, 168
Scherschel, Joe, 72; and radio control of cameras, 79; photograph by, 73; and special equipment to photograph motion, 72, 74
Schneider, Al, 80; description of equipment for special problems of LIFE photographers, 72-80
Schneider, Romy, 97
Schulthess, Emil, 42; photograph by, 42
Schweikardt, Eric, photograph by, 143
Sealab I, 77; photographic coverage of, 78
Sequence photographs, 131, 136, 138-139
Shadows, photography of, 84-85, 182-183
Shakbut bin Sultan, 13
Shoemaker, William S., 159
Shull, Henry A., 200-201
Shutter(s): corrosion of, 32; effect of cold environments on, 22, 36; holes in, 96; malfunctions of, 108, 118-119; noise of, 94; speeds of, and photography of motion, 72, 74, 129-130, 131, 136; synchronization of, with strobe lights, 110-111, 112, 118, 119; tests for, 108-109, 113
Silica gel, 17, 19, 30
Silk, George: photographs by, 136-137, 140-141, 151, 152; and sports photography, 136, 140, 151, 152
Single-lens reflex, and photographing over heads of crowds, 66-67
Slit camera, 134, 140, 146; photographs taken with, 140-141, 146
Smith, Robert, and sports photography, 132-133
Snead, Sam, 94
Snow, effects of, on exposure, 23
Snyder, Joel: and fog-illusion filter, 82; photograph by, 83
Southern Illinois University, 158
Special effects by breaking rules, 175-202; backlighting, 196-197, 198-199; blending of colors, 200-201; blur from greased filter, 190, 191; blur from inferior lens, 200-201; blur by selective focus, 192, 193; color shift, 194-195, 202; cropping, 186-187; day into night, 196-197; diffraction of light, 190; elimination of detail, 175, 178-179, 180-181, 198-199; fog effect, 82, 83; graininess, 176, 178-179; high contrast, 180-181, 184-185; multiple exposures, 88-89, 176-177; perspective distortion, 177, 188-189; sandwiching, 177; shadows, 84-85, 182-183; silhouettes, 175, 178-179, 198-199; "stars," 190; unusual angle, 175. See also Equipment for special problems; Motion, photography of
Split-field lens, 60-61
Sports photography, 132-133, 134-154
"Stars," 190; filter to create, 190
Stop-action photography, 128-131, 134-135, 136-137, 138-139, 142-143, 144-145, 147, 148-149, 152; and camera angle, 130, 152; and

distance, 130; and panning, 130-131, 148; and peak action, 129-130, 142; and sequence photographs, 131, 136
Streaks, on contact print, *123;* significance of, 123
Strobe lights, electronic: double-pole double-throw momentary contact switch for, 72, *73,* 74; incorrect wiring for, 93-94; remote radio control for, *78;* sequential rotary switches for, *74;* and stop-action photography, 129, 144; synchronization of, with shutter, 110-111, 112, 118, 119
Sund, Harald, 178; photographs by, *175, 178-179*
Switches: double-pole double-throw momentary contact switch, 72, *73,* 74; sequential rotary switch, *74*
Synchronization of shutter with strobe, 110-111, 112; symptoms of malfunction of, 118, *119*

Synchro-Tester, *112*
Szczygielski, Anthony, 187; photographs by, *186, 187*

Temperature, effect of, on film. *See* Cold environments; Hot environments
Tension on film, symptoms of excess, *114*
Test(s): focusing system, 112, *113;* lens diaphragm, 108, *109;* lens resolution, 104-106, *107;* shutter speed, 108, *109, 113;* synchronization of shutter with strobe lights, *110-111, 112*
Test charts for lenses, *105, 107*
Thall, Garry, 169; photograph by, *169*
Thompson, Ed, 92
Timers for motorized cameras, 76, *77,* 78; cost of, 77
Triolo, Tony, photograph by, *73*
Tripod: motor-driven head for, 74, *75,* 76; substitutes for, 95

Trouble-shooting cameras, 104-124. *See also* Defects appearing on contact sheet
Twin-lens reflex, and photographing over heads of crowds, 66

Ultraviolet light, effect on color rendition of film, 23, 39
Ultrawide (camera), 62
Umbrella: in hot environments, 96; in wet environments, 20

Video Color Negative Analyzer, 160, *161*
Vignetting, *116;* significance of, 114, 116
Viki, *96-97,* 98

Waist-level viewer, 66, *67*
Walch, Bob, 45; demonstration of elimination of reflections, *52-53*
Walker, Hank, *24*
Washburn, Bradford,

photograph by, *11*
Waterproof camera housings, 20-21
Wayman, Stan, 15; photograph by, *16*
Weather. *See* Cold environments; Dry environments; Hot environments; Humid environments; Wet environments
Weston, Edward, 172
Wet environments: effects of, on cameras and film, 20-21, 32; effects of, on exposure meters, 20, 32; photographs taken in, *30-31, 32-33;* protection of equipment from, *18,* 20-21, 31, 35. *See also* Humid environments
White, Minor, photograph by, *cover*
Wide-angle pictures, elimination of barrel distortion in, *62-63*
Wills, Maury, *138-139*
Wilson, Tom, 162

Zimmerman, John, ·144; photograph by, *144-145*